Zen

Tales from the Journey

Scott Shaw

Buddha Rose Publications

ISBN: 1-877792-43-8
ISBN-13: 9781877792434

First Edition 2007
Second Edition 2009
Third Edition 2018
Fourth Edition 2026

Library of Congress Control Number: 2008941256

10 9 8 7 6 5 4 3 2 1

Printed in the United States of America

Zen

Tales from the Journey

Table of Contents

Introduction   **7**

1 *Krishnamurti and the Bee Sting of Satori*   **9**

2 *Shama Baba*   **17**

3 *Surrender*   **43**

4 *Consciousness*   **49**

5 *Energy and the Spiritual Path*   **58**

6 *Where Myths Are Born*   **75**

7 *On the Inside Looking Out*   **79**

8 *Enlightenment is Easy. It's Life That's Hard.* **87**

9 *What is a Cult Leader?*   **93**

10 *The Conflict of "I" and the Spiritual Path*   **99**

11 *Open Eye Meditation*   **118**

12 *I Was Born in L.A.*   **140**

13 *Who is Spiritual?*   **144**

14 *"I Know More Than You!"*   **157**

15 *The Dynamics of Transition*   **165**

16 *Magical Thinking*   **171**

17 *The Student Becomes the Master*   **175**

18 *Don't Get Lost in the Tranquility*   **179**

19 *The Pathway to Enlightenment*   **186**

20 *It's All in the Giving*   **191**

Introduction

The essays that make up this book were written over the past decade. The experiences that laid the foundations for them were lived over the past three or four.

As I always tell people, *"My reality cannot be your reality, just as your reality cannot be mine."*

With this as a basis for understand, this book is designed to provide you, the reader, with a perception of *The Spiritual Path*—as I have encountered it. It is my hope that these words may provide some inspiration, possible guidance, and maybe a smile or two for those of you who, like I, try to find deeper meaning and to make sense out of this place we call, *"Life."*

It is essential to note, however, in this book I am not telling anyone how they should live, what they should think, or how they should experience life. I am simply presenting some of the experience that have made up my life, intermingled with the realizations that grew from them, with the hope that they may help you remove some of the obstacles to your own personal growth and spiritual development.

S.
5 June 2007
Tokyo, Japan

Chapter 1

Krishnamurti
and the Bee Sting of Satori

During the later stages of his life, the great sage, J. Krishnamurti would periodically give informal lectures at his center in Ojai, California. In the late 1970's, though I was a university student, I was much more focused upon the spiritual life than my studies. So, whenever one of these lectures would take place, I would forgo my classes and travel to Ojai.

It was a truly spiritual process for me. I would rise early, consciously bathe—washing away Karmic blemishes and the physical constraints of this material existence. Then, I would get dressed, meditate, and finally, climb onto my motorcycle and, with the wind blowing through my hair, make the hundred-mile journey Northward.

The talks were given in a tree-covered field at the Krishnamurti Foundation. Usually about twenty to thirty people would attend. So, it was very intimate.

Each morning, as the people would slowly begin to congregate, we would sit on the grass awaiting his arrival. Most of the attending were his direct devotees—though he never liked that delineation. Me, I was a Dharma Bum, on the path of spiritual awakening.

In the waiting, some people conversed, while others would cross their legs, close their eyes, and meditate. Myself, long believing that one of the most integral elements of meditation could only be accomplished with your eyes open, would sit by myself and experience all of the visual stimuli which could be taken in at this site Krishnamurti had called one of his homes for decades.

Then, he would appear—this aging Indian born sage. Who, like the Buddha, had renounced divinity—stating that no religion and no individual could bring you the truth. It could only be found within.

Order of the Star
Decades before, he had disbanded *the Order of the Star*. This organization had been created by Annie Besant and Charles Webster Leadbeater. These two individuals were leading members of Madam Blavatsky's *Theosophical Society* who had created *the Order of the Star* in order to propagate that Krishnamurti was *Lord Maitreya—the World Teacher* who had been predicted in the Pali Canon. They taught that Krishnamurti would lead the world onto a new level of spirituality.

In actuality, this is what he did. He left all of the nonsense of holiness behind.

With this selfless action of renunciation, he illustrated that he truly was an enlightened being of the highest caliber—teaching for no reason other than that of the spiritual realization of humanity.

Unassuming, Krishnamurti would wear slacks, a plain button up shirt, and usually a sweater. His silver hair was combed over to cover his baldness. It glistened in the sun. His divine presence was indisputable.

Journey to Ojai
One morning, as I was preparing to make the journey to Ojai, a friend of mine from University

showed up at my door. Not to be unkind, but he was a rather curious fellow. One of those people that when you would say something to him, perhaps five minutes later it would sink in and then they would answer.

He was a rock drummer, in love with the music of *The Grateful Dead,* and the drug orientated byproducts of that obsession. As to whether or not his mind had always been lost to the realms of distance, I do not know. But, for the period of time I knew him, he was, *Spaced-Out.*

As he was one of those people who would come over and sit for hour after hour, never leaving until he was directly guided out the door, he was, obviously, quite interested in what I was doing and where I was going. I told him, and his mind was made up, he was going to come along.

Normally, I would have heartily invited anyone who possessed even the slightest interest to make the journey with me to sit at the feet of Krishnamurti. Somehow, in this case, however, I knew he was not the right person to take along.

All my efforts to discourage his accompaniment failed. So, we climbed into his 1970's green Fiat station wagon and we were off.

We arrived with little incident and sat down in the field with the others who had come to listen to the words of Krishnamurti. The Master arrived. He sat down in his chair and began to speak.

The Bees

One of the common occurrences in the springtime in Ojai was that there were quite a few bees buzzing around the lecture site. This day was no different. In the many times I had been there, I had never seen anyone get stung, however. Well, that was all about to change...

"Ouch!" my friend screams, as Krishnamurti is in the midst of his discourse.

Yes, there I was, sitting ten feet from Krishnamurti, one foot from my friend, and he was screaming, *"Ouch!" "Ouch, I got stung by a bee!"*

Now, all the thoughts that would normally race through anyone's mind raced through mine, *"Maybe Krishnamurti will think that I don't know this guy." "But no, he is sitting closer to me than anyone else. And, as there are not that many people here. He has to know!" "Man, if I had gotten stung, I would not have screamed. I would have just held it in."*

Through all of the mental calisthenics, which were going on in my mind, I kept my focus on Krishnamurti. Except for a brief moment of silence, when the initial yell rang out, he never stopped his lecture.

How profound, I understood. It immediately brought me back to my center. The average person may have inquired as to the nature and condition of a single person's injury. But, that would take away from the greater good—from all of those sitting in his presence, absorbing what he had to say.

My friend sat there ranting, until I told him he really needed to be quiet. Krishnamurti did not flinch.

The Center of Attention

This is one of the leading problems with the human condition. People want to be the center of attention. They desire focus to be placed solely upon themselves—sympathy for their trials and tribulations. *Physical Self* is only *Physical Self,* however.

Nobody can feel what you feel but you. Understanding this, you must come to the ultimate conclusion that what you are going through is what you are going through.

Certainly, in lesser circumstances, attention can be given to individual needs. But, in the grand scheme of the evolving consciousness of humanity, a single bee sting is of little overall importance. How you deal with your bee stings, however, delineates your level of interactive consciousness. And, your consciousness must be acutely interactive, with the cosmic whole, if you desire to raise it to the level where *Nirvana* may be encountered.

Story Telling

I recently told this story to a friend of mine. She immediately chimed in; *"It's all about ego. Your ego was damaged because your friend was screaming. Your friend's ego was hurt because a bee stung him. Krishnamurti's ego was telling him, 'Why is this guy yelling during my lecture.'"*

Though laughingly dumbfounded by her initial assessment of the situation, it did make me realize how we each perceive life from our own level of evolution. This is the basis for *Satori.* If you are locked into focusing solely upon the perception of your own ego and your own *Physical Self,* then you can never, *"Release"* and experience *Cosmic Consciousness.*

Therefore, you must base your movement towards enlightenment on the understanding that we are all physical beings, with the limitations of human perceptions. By stepping beyond these limitations is what causes all of us to encounter *Satori.*

Motorcycle Satori

During this same period of time, I remember one spring evening when I was twenty years old. I had nothing really to do and nowhere really to go. But, I knew I needed to be, *"Out."* So, I climbed onto my motorcycle and begin to ride around the hills of the West San Fernando Valley.

As I rode, something came over me. It was not the freedom commonly associated with riding a motorcycle, it was something much deeper. I began to transcend the limitation of my *Physical Self,* which I had been so keenly focused upon that particular day.

To make a long story short—I rode through the hills, as a totally blissful sensation began to overtake me. An experience that escapes words.

Like some divine force guided me, I began to close my eyes as I continued to ride. I embraced the pure white light.

I rode on for what seemed like forever. Every now and then I would open my eyes and see that I was traveling down the street, exactly where I should be. This blissful ride, with my eyes mostly closed, went on for maybe an hour or so. Then, as if coming down off a drug high, I began to reconnect with my *Physical Self.* My eyes naturally began to remain open for longer and longer periods. Though I tried, I could not recapture the feeling. So, I eventually headed for home.

Note: As this occurrence was a manifestation of the physical life I call my own. And, as each person walks a different path and their life is orchestrated to their own needs—it is essential to keep in mind, never try to imitate what another person has lived. In other words, "Don't try this at home."

Atman and Brahman

Physical Self is only *Physical Self*. *Physical Self* is not *Higher Self*. This is why consciousness is divided into two differing levels: *Atman* and *Brahman—Individual Self* and *Universal Self*.

If you maintain your focus upon Individual Self: your wants, your needs, your desires, your pain, and your suffering, you can never transcend the limitations of *Individual Self* and merge with the *Cosmic Whole*. For this reason, an individual on *the Spiritual Path* begins to move their consciousness away from the momentary affliction, which plague the *Individual Self* and formally transform their consciousness to the more profound realms of understanding.

Life is life and some things hurt. This is a part of the human condition. Lying about it, to yourself or others, is not the resolution of this issue. Transcendence, however, is the path to overcoming the limitation of *Self*. Krishnamurti knew it—he kept speaking.

A Pathway to Satori

For the individual, on the pathway to enlightenment, getting stung by a bee, while a transcendent individual such as Krishnamurti was speaking, would have induced an instant dose of *Satori*.

Satori, that sudden burst of enlightenment that can happen anywhere, at any time.

I mean, how profound—getting stung by a bee while in the presence of an enlightened being. This would instantly shift anyone out of normal consciousness. What more could you ask for?

For *Satori* to be encountered, however, you must be void of *Individual Self*—or at least willing to shift out of the mode of *Individual Self.* This is why, for centuries, the Masters of Zen have guided the students to ponder the *Koan.* A *Koan* is an abstract statement that shifts the mind from the bounds of known reality.

By performing this meditative action, the *Thinking Mind* encounters new realms of consciousness not encountered by the average individual. This is why Zen is vastly different from other schools of *Meditative Consciousness*—it trains the mind to formally embrace the abstract—consciously. From this, the restrains of everyday thinking gradually fall away and the experience of *Satori* is encountered.

Enlightenment is Everywhere

Many people believe that the only path to enlightenment is through meditation. They are wrong. Enlightenment is available everywhere. You just have to be open to the process and willing to let it enter you from wherever you find yourself—riding a motorcycle, getting stung by a bee, or sitting in meditation.

The trials and tribulations of life are a great source point for *Satori.* With each obstacle, or bee sting, you can either get upset, focus your consciousness on the limitations of the physical world, and remove yourself from the realms of enlightenment. Or, you can witness how ridiculous this place we call life is and embrace the perfect beauty of it.

Open up, see the beauty, embrace the perfection, and your bee stings will be your path to Nirvana.

Chapter 2
Shama Baba

I met Shama Baba on one of those warm overcast winter New Delhi mornings when you're not quite sure why the sun isn't shining because the atmosphere is radiating with solar energy. It was on Asaf Ali Road—the artery that divides Old Delhi from New Delhi. I was walking down the street. And, I mean this literally, as there were far too many people sleeping in the doorways that lined sidewalk, to make any positive headway if I had not moved my pathway to the street.

Awh India, the land of overpopulation, poverty, starvation, death, and enlightenment.

I stopped for a moment and looked across the street, which seemed to have instantly become very-very busy. I was pondering the best place to make my crossing, when a very dark-skinned man, wearing traditional white Indian clothing, walked up to me. He had shortly cropped white hair and a beard. With him was this beautiful little girl with the biggest eyes—she must have been about five years old.

"Where are you going Baba," he asked.

"Baba," a term which is so commonly assigned to Westerners in India. I felt unworthy. I was only eighteen years old.

"Are you going to Bodh Gaya," he continued.

"How strange," I thought. *"How did he know?"* I looked at him and nodded, *"Yes."*

Bodh Gaya, the place where the Buddha found his enlightenment under the Bodhi Tree.

"We come from Varanasi," the man continued.

For those of you who may not know, Varanasi is the closest urban center to Bodh Gaya.

"All of our luggage was stolen on the train and we've had very little to eat. Could you give me some money to buy food for the little one, Baba?"

For a moment the thought did go through my mind, *"Perhaps he really was from Varanasi and maybe his luggage had been stolen."* But, I quickly dismissed that idea having been duly overwhelmed by the massive amounts of India's poverty and people asking me for money everywhere I stepped.

Though I truly wished I could help the whole country, I didn't have the financial resources to feed all of India. I continued to stare across the street, hoping that the man may catch the hint and leave. He did not.

I walked a few feet away from him, basically to see his reaction. He stood firm—the little girl holding his hand while she also stared at me.

I looked at my watch. I was actuality waiting for the local bank to open so I could exchange some U.S. currency into Rupees. It was that time. So, I recommence my walk.

As I begin to walk away, the man once again asked if I would give him some money. I stopped, reached into my pocket, and gave him all the change I had. He happily said,

"Thank you, Baba. Thank you so much."
"No problem, Baba," I replied as I walked on.

After I had made the necessary exchanges in the bank, I spent the rest of the day roaming the streets of Old Delhi. The visuals of the timeworn buildings, the people everywhere, the cows, the cars, the bicycles, and the holy men—it is just overwhelmingly beautiful for those of us with an abstract sense of the aesthetic.

As I walked the streets, the thought of the man and the little girl with the beautiful eyes, frequently came to my mind. *"Was he really from Varanasi or just another lost soul asking for money?" "Should I have given him more money for the sake of the little girl?"* Something unexplained had touched me. But, as I later realized, I was far too caught up in the way things were supposed to be to see anything clearly at that point in my life.

I walked until about 3:00 PM. Then, I headed back to my hotel. I was still very jet-lagged. So, by that time of the day, I was ready for sleep.

Brahmamurta
Back in my hotel, I quickly went to sleep. The next morning, I awoke. It was still dark outside. I looked at the clock. It was exactly, 4:30 AM.

My first thought was, *"This is way too early."* But then I immediately realized, *"Wait, its Brahmamurta. I should meditate."*

A very abstract thought hit me at that moment, however, *"When it's Brahmamurta in*

India, it is another time somewhere else. So, what does Brahmamurta really means?"

I concluded that this realization was probably just more of an excuse not sit and meditate than anything else. So, I decided to write in my journal instead.

Time passed, sunlight came through my window, and the day began. I went outside. The smell of morning India hot me as it always had. It is a very hard scent to describe. Yet, very distinctive. The air is permeated with the aroma of all those millions of people using cow dung for fuel and the streets and the alleys for bathrooms. Awh, India...

On the street I hailed a three-wheel taxi, jumped in, and was off to the Post Office to mail a few letters back to Los Angeles. I arrived, but the Post Office would not be opened for another hour. So, I decided to walk around and surveying the New Delhi morning. I choose a street at random and began to follow it. I watched a family of Sikhs, who lived underneath tarps attached to their two taxicabs, embrace the morning and wash their long hair with water that flowed from some unknown source, but skirted the street. I witnessed a long-haired, long-bearded *Sadhu* sitting in the middle of the roadway, (literally in the middle of the street), lost deep in the realms of meditation. A loving cow stood guard over him as the cars raced past. I saw a family of five speeding past me—all riding aboard the same motor scooter. The father wildly drove in and out of traffic. I watched a Rolls Royce fly down the road with no care for who or what came in its path. And, again, I saw the poverty, the really poor with no hope but religion, no solace but the dream of a higher incarnation—life at the edge of life, where only the enlightened can be freed.

Corrinath Place

The Post Office opened—my mailings were complete. I headed over to Corrinath Place. Corrinath Place is the section of Delhi where rows of shops line the streets set up for the amusement of tourist. But, if you are willing to play the game of South Asian price haggling, you can get a few necessary travel items for a good price.

I purchased what I needed for the continuation of my journey. I was scheduled to be traveling Southward, on a train that evening.

I had time, the day was young, and so was I. So, I decided to go and sit in the park, central to Corrinath Place. This park could be a location of refuge in this nonstop, overpopulated, over trafficked city. Unfortunately, as is the norm, I was confronted by individuals who wanted to clean my ears with dirty Q-tips and men who wanted to give me a massage.

This one masseuse came up. I keep saying, *"No,"* but he kept rubbing my shoulders, stating, *"You'll like it, you'll see. Very cheap."* I kept pulling free, repeated, *"No Thanks."* But, he would move with me, reposition himself, and rub some more.

Then, off in the distance, I saw the man with the little girl, who I had met the day before. In that same instant, his eyes met mine, and he begins to walk towards me with a big smile on his face. I was glad to see anyone who could make this man stop massaging.

"Hello Baba," he said.
"Please Baba, come and sit with me," I replied.

He and his little girl sat down. He smiled and asked me if I wanted the man to stop. I told him I did.

He scolded the man in Hindi. The masseuse gave him a strange look, stopped, got up, and immediately walked away.

"Thank you, Baba," I said.

He was smiling as he looked deeply into my eyes—too deeply. I had to turn away. The stare was too intense. I focused on the little girl. Her gigantic eyes looked very sad. With all of my inner-city kid skepticism, I sadly have to say that I wondered if she had been trained to look like that way.

Then instantly, like being hit by an unseen wave, he spoke,

"Your desires are not clear. You think one thing but want another. That's why you are having trouble following your destiny. All you have to do is ask for what you want, and you will receive it. Like the man giving you a massage. You were not firm."

"Interesting point," I thought.

We sat for a time and then he said,

"Baba, you are a very generous man."

I was happy the subject had changed. My mind went to the money I had given him the day before. In fact, I felt a little guilty for I had only given him a few Rupees the day before.

He asked when would I be leaving for Varanasi. I told him that I would be leaving that evening.

Out of nowhere, like it wasn't me who was talking, I said,

"I know you must want to return to Varanasi. Let me pay for you and your daughter's ticket."

He looked at me very seriously and said,

"Sadhus ride for free."

We looked deep into each other's eyes—for one of those seconds that seem to last an eternity. A million thoughts raced through my mind. They were interrupted, he continued,

"But, I will take the same train as you."

Before I could even comprehend what had just occurred, he asked if I had some extra money for food for the little girl. I reached in my pocket and gave him a handful of Rupees.

As they walked off, I could not help but think, *"Oh sure, you're going to be on the train tonight."*

I watched them walk away. Then, before any other ear cleaners, masseuses, or traveling salesman selling prayer beads, pictures of deities, or hashish could approach me, I too got up and left the park.

As I headed back towards my hotel in a three-wheeled taxi, the afternoon air of Delhi was changing from the smell of burning cow dung to that of pure automobile exhaust: the cars, the scooters, the trucks, literally bumping into one another—going nowhere fast. My thoughts shifted from the traffic to the promise of impending bliss awaiting me in Bodh Gaya. As my mind wandered, at an intersection, my driver had apparently performed some wrong act. A rifle wearing Sikh policeman walked up. He was yelling in Hindi. Then, he literally smacked the driver in the head. The driver attempting to explain himself, was smacked again, and again. Then, he was told to get going.

India, one of the holiest places on Earth...

Back at my hotel, I packed, checked out, grabbed a taxi, and arrived at the train station about two hours early. The only rush was in my own mind—feed by my nervousness about my ability to actually make it through Delhi's insane traffic and to the train station on time.

The Train Ride

As my taxi drove up, the night began to close in. Men, women, children, entire families began moving into their designated corners of the train station. They proceed to lay down their few possessions and unroll their blankets. I wondered, *"How anyone could sleep here? It was so noisy."* But then, I rationalized that it was at least shelter. I supposed one could get used to the noise.

I sat in the station, waiting for my train, watching the people. A young Sikh came up and asked me in English if I knew the time. It was 8:22 PM.

A young *Sadhu,* maybe thirteen or fourteen years old, wandered the station. He said nothing, yet people came up to him, performing *Namaskar Asana, "Hands in prayer position,"* and gave him money.

India, a country that worships poverty. The Sadhu—the poorest and the most holy of holy.

I had long understood that each culture makes the most of what it has and then places it on a pedestal. America—wealth and power is everything. India—it's spirituality and its poverty. The most impoverished man is the most holy man.

24

I looked out across the station—literally jammed with people. But, I was the only Westerner. I felt very alone.

Here they all were—all that I had imagined. Yet, the harshness of India was a far cry from the idealism I possessed when I was sixteen years old with the unrealistic desire of renouncing the world and living in a cave in the Himalayas for the rest of my earthy existence.

As I sat there, my thoughts traveled to my Indian friend and his little girl with the big brown eyes. *"Where was he? Undoubtedly, out sleeping somewhere with no thought of me,"* I imagined.

About this time, I began to get really thirsty. So, I stood up and went in search of something to drink. There was yellowish water running from a continuous faucet that drained into a big porcelain basin. But, I was not about to drink that. The snack stand was closed. What was I to do? *Tapasia "Spiritual purification,"* I thought. This will be my *Tapasia* for the evening. I must deal with my thirst. So, I curbed my desire and sat back down.

The time ticked by very slowly. But, my train's departure time was approaching. So, I walked onto the designated platform and waited for its arrival.

An orange-robed *Sanyassin, "Swami,"* walked by me, saying, *"Hey Sita, Hey Ram,"* with his begging hand extended. I looked closer at him and realized he was a Westerner—probably European.

My immediate thought was, *"Is this spirituality? This man, from a wealthy country, putting pressure on the already distressed economy of India? No, it was not!"* But, the local people were giving him money.

The questions and confusion began to race through my mind, *"Was this the spirituality I was seeking?" "Why was I here?" "This place is terrible; so much poverty, so many people, so much violence in the streets."*

Most of all, I couldn't understand the train announcements in jumbled Hindi. I became very concerned about missing my train. Finally, I composed myself and walked up to a man waiting on the platform. He was an, obviously, very refined, East India man. I asked him what was being said.

There I was, a long-haired, bearded American *Yogi* asking assistance from a very formal East Indian man, wearing a very expensive suit. It was obviously that he wished I would not bother him. But, he was nice enough, and as was waiting for the same train, he promised he would let me know which track I would find it upon. The train arrived. My newfound train-ridding compatriot guided me to it. I found my car and compartment. *First Class Sleeper.* I entered.

There were three of us to share the compartment: a local businessman, balding, maybe forty or so, an aging Sikh, fifty-five plus, and myself. One of the four bunks would remain empty.

When we're all inside the porter came in and asked the other two men in Hindi, *"Was it okay that they were in a compartment with an American?"* I must admit, I took offense at this. But, *none-the-less*, there were no complaints. We all settled in and the trained pulled out into the India Subcontinent night.

As the train began to move down the tracks, I looked out the window onto the platform for my newfound Indian friend and the little girl. There was no sign of them. I laughed to myself, thinking, *"I knew they would not be on the train."*

As my consciousness returned to my compartment, it was a bit strange to be in a small-enclosed space with two men I did not know. But they were more than friendly, however, both spoke fluent English. We discussed our appropriate missions in life: the businessman to do some business in Lucknow, (one of the stops on the way to Varanasi), the Sikh to visit a sister, and me, to travel to one of the most holy places on Earth, bath in the River Ganges, and sit where Siddhartha Guatama, the Sakyamuni Buddha sat, under the Bodhi Tree.

Post some basic discourse, and some nighttime *Cha "Tea,"* delivered by the porter, it was time to pull down the bunks and go to sleep. I was assigned the upper bunk. This was, no doubt, due to my comparatively young age. The businessman took off his clothing, hung up his suit, and retired in his underwear. The Sikh, obviously use to the finer things in life, had the porter help him into his pajamas. Me, I just slept in the clothing I wore. I was still a bit uncomfortable with all this newfound camaraderie.

As we settled in, the Sikh opened up his book of scriptures. As I looked down from my top bunk, I noticed that inside the cover was a copy of a South Asian adult magazine with semi-nude girls. I was very amused. Certainly, not as flamboyant as its Western counterpart. The magazine, *none-the-less,* detailed the essence of this man's disposition.

As the rails vibrated on, I slept little that evening—emerged in the thoughts of India, being in a compartment with two loudly snoring men who I did not know, and what would I find in Bodh Gaya.

The early morning sun, essence of the Hindu deity *Surya,* eventual shown in through our compartments window and I was saved from my sleepless night. I looked out at the rapidly passing scenery and saw the immense landscape of central India—the ravaged land, the minimal crops, and the people attempting to find a means of survival on the early morning pastures that had been robbed of minerals ages ago.

The vision of the orange glow of morning Mother India was breathtaking.

The train's first stop was Lucknow. Lucknow, where British Lords and military had set up shop a century before. Now all were gone. All that remains were droves of people existing on this once fertile plain, which now pulsated within an industrialized city.

My two cabin friends were on their way. I too got off the train for a few moments and walked around a bit. I searched, but no sign of my friend or his little girl. The train bell sounded. I got back on, and the journey continued.

As the day passed, left alone in my cabin, I was lost between wanting to see every inch of Mother India and the periodic catnaps I fell into due to my remaining jetlag and lack of sleep from the previous night. Eventually, in a seemingly endless day, the train arrived in Varanasi. I got my bag, and with best wishes from all the train crew, out the door I went.

Varanasi

Almost instantly, I noticed my friend. He was walking towards me with a big smile on his face, as if he knew that I thought he had not made the journey. He calmly walks up,

"Did you have a nice ride, Baba?"
"It was all right," I cautiously answered.

28

I did not see the little girl, so I asked where she was. He pointed down the platform and there she was with her hand stuck out accepting alms.

Many unexplained things had happened on this journey already. Still, I was a little surprised to see him. I stood there for a few moments in a bit of a daze.

He said, *"Let's go, Baba."*

So, we started to walk. The little girl ran to catch up. We exited to the front of the station.

Varanasi is a very different city than Delhi. *None-the-less*, as is common in South Asia, tons of taxi drivers were there offering to take me anywhere I wanted to go. They walked up, tried to grab my bag from my hand. They said, *"Hashish," "Girls."* But, I held tight, often times, forcefully having to pull my suitcase from their clutches.

My associate stood there and watched in amusement. He asked,
"When are you going to Bodh Gaya?"
I said, *"I thought I would stay here in Varanasi for a day or so."*
"That's good," he quickly answered, *"You need to calm your mind. You think too much about the way things are supposed to be. Go to Mata Ganga, (the Ganges River), and purify."*

"Who does he think he is," was my first thought. But, before I could say anything...

"Oh, by the way, Baba, do you have some small money for the little one to eat?"

I looked at him. A very funny feeling came over me. In one sense, I laughed, for here was this man asking me for money after going so far. What did he do, go on the train ride just for fun? Was he now going back to Delhi? What is he all about? Yet, while looking at him, a peace permeated my being. An inner peace I had never experienced.

What could I do? I reached in my pocket, and I pulled out some Rupees and I gave them to him.

"Oh, thank you, Baba. You are so generous."

Then, he and the little girl walked away. In a seeming instant, he and the little girl faded into the crowd. Again, I was alone. I stood there pondering life. But, taxi drivers and their young helpers grabbing at my bag quickly disrupted my thoughts.

Finally, I walked up to a seemingly disinterested driver, sitting in his car, and asked him to take me to my hotel. After a bit of haggling over the price, reluctantly, he drove me to my hotel.

By the time I checked in, it was late afternoon. I was still jet-lagged and tired from the night before. But, I knew I was in India for one reason. So, out to the street I went—in search of transportation to *Mata Ganga.*

Mata Ganga

A three-wheeled bicycle taxi guy immediately pedaled up.

"Need a ride to the Ganges, Baba?"

Everybody seemingly knowing where I was going and what I was doing was really beginning to work on me. But, I climbed onboard and we made our way through the Varanasi traffic.

The driver was a friendly enough guy. He told me about his family and how someday he hoped to own one of the three wheeled motorized taxis. Finally, we arrived.

Due to the traffic, both motorized and on foot, common to the passageway to the holiest of rivers, he parked back several hundred yards. I was pointed in the direction of the Ganges and told he would wait for me. *"No, you don't have to do that."* But, he insisted.

As I walked through the crowds, a strange sense of absolute reality came upon me. Not so much of a *"Peak Experience"* but more just a very powerful sense of a one-pointedness of mind and reality—everyone was there for the same reason.

I walked down the steps to the Ganges just as the sun was about to set. There were thousands of people there. Some were in the water. Some standing by this holy river. Some doing laundry. Some meditating.

It is an intense feeling, which escapes words, when so many people are focusing all of their energy on this one source of divine life and liberation.

I walked down to her banks of *Mata Ganga.* I touched the water and rubbed some on my *Ajna Chakra, "Third Eye."*

There I was, in the heart of Hinduism, surrounded by pundits, disciples, worshipers, and sacred cows. I sat for a while on the banks, attempting to take it all in.

Over in the distance, I noticed an aged man, seated upon a throne. Many people surrounding him. My initial thought was that he must be a *Guru;* someone very important. I walked over to see him.

As I got closer, I realized he was not moving. *Meditating,* was my first thought. But no, he was dead. He had been brought to the river to be given back to the Mother—the source of all creation.

As the sun set, he was taken out in a small barge and released to *Mata Ganga.* The Ganges River, the holiest place to live, the most sacred place to die.

As the evening came on, I was surprised that my friend and his little girl had not shown up. They seemed to be everywhere else that I was. I looked around but there was no sign of them, only the men dressed as *Sadhus* trying to sell me hashish.

Prayer Beads

It was getting dark, so I made my way back towards where the bicycle taxi guy was apparently waiting. I passed a man who had a small cart and was selling *Malas, "Prayer beads."* How could I pass this up? A *Mala* from the Ganges.

I looked through them, picked out a few, and asked how much. He only wanted two Rupees for the several I had chosen. An amount so small, it was hard to fathom—like less than half a U.S. cent. I handed him a large bill. A bill that would be equivalent to about ten-dollars U.S. I mean, they were worth it and I wanted to help the guy out. But, he began to make me change. The more I tried to tell him to keep it, the more he insisted on giving it to me.

"Baba, the man does not want money. He only wants to survive in the presence of Mata Ganga."

I turned. My friend had arrived—*hand-in-hand* with his little girl.

32

"But, I want to help him out, Baba."
"You already have. You cannot give somebody something they do not want."

With that, I took the change being offered. The *Mala* maker smiled.

As detailed, it was almost as if I had expected my friend to show up. When he did, our interaction occurred without a second thought to his presence. As I looked back on this moment, I thought how strange this was, for I was not normally this open to people I did not know.

The three of us, walked off through the crowds.

As we walked, a strange thought came to me. I did not even know this man's name. After the thoughts raced through my mind for a seeming eternity about just how to ask, finally I blurted it out, *"Baba, what should I call you?"*

He stopped and looked at me as if he had never heard such an absurd question. After several moments, he smiled and said,

"Once, a long time ago, people would call me, Shama. But I don't really know why."

Before I could even think about his answer, he immediately continued,

"Baba, do you have some small money I could have for the little one to eat?"

Without a thought, I pulled ten rupees from my pocket and gave it to him. He said,

"Thank you, Baba, you are so generous." He began to walk away.

As he did, he continued,

"I've never understood why people try to name feelings and put a name on things."

He stops his progression, turned, and looked at me,

"You know they only exist in our dreams, like the Mata Ganga."

Without skipping a beat, he walked into the masses and was gone.

A bit lost in attempting to make sense about whom this man was, what I was doing in India, and where my bicycle taxi driver was waiting, I walked on—somewhat like a zombie.

Soon I heard, *"Baba, Baba, here I am."* My driver was calling out to me.

The Rock of Satori

I mounted the back of his bicycle taxi and we were again on our way. He peddled through the early evening streets of Varanasi. My mind was lost in the realms of pondering spirituality, when all of sudden, BAM! Someone had tossed a rock at me and hit me in the back of my shoulder. *"Ouch!"* It hurt!

You know, this is the paradox of India. A mystical land of peace, enlightenment, and unprovoked acts of violence.

The driver stopped and asked if I was Okay. Me, I looked around to see who had done it. Of course, they had retreated into the crowds, unwilling to confront me *face-to-face*. Most of all I knew I was lucky that the large rock didn't hit me in the head. Because it was really thrown hard. After a few moments, we drove on.

The driver explained that many people don't like Westerners. They think we destroyed true India. Maybe it is true, I do not know. All I knew is that it was not me. I was not part of the British Empire. And, my shoulder really hurt.

Days of Limka

As we traveled back towards my hotel, I began to feel very nauseous. The plight of India had begun to set in.

At the hotel, back in my room, I bathed—washed away, as best as I could, the scraped skin on my back. Then, I quickly faded into sleep. The sleep did not last long, however, as dysentery had begun to set in. I spent the night in mystery.

With the rise of the sun, I was still very sick. Too sick to go out. I spent the day, and the next day, and the next locked in my room—calling room service and asking for new rolls of toilet paper. The only thing I could put into my body was the local drink, *Limka*—a kind of a carbonated lemon-lime beverage.

The days passed slowly—sleep became boring and overdone. There was no T.V. and only the traditional music from *Radio India* to listen to. I had no books to read and had written every nuance of every experience I could remember in my journal. Meditation was out of the question. I was way too sick. So, I lay there in bed thinking, *"Oh this is great, I come to India for enlightenment, instead I am going to die!"*

By sunrise of the third day, though still very sick, I knew I had to get out. So, I dragged myself up, put on my clothing, and made it to the lobby of my hotel. My intended destination, Bodh Gaya. Siddhartha Guatama found enlightenment there. I hoped I could just get a little healthier.

Bodh Gaya

The Hotel doorman hailed me a taxi. I got in and we were on our way. As we passed the gates of the hotel, I saw my bicycle taxi driver looking at me like why wasn't I using him. I waved and we drove on.

Bodh Gaya is several miles outside of Varanasi. The drive is nice as it is a very gradual progression from the traffic and intense population of Hinduism's most holy city to the fields of Mother India. The drive to me was a time of inner reflection. Here I finally was in the final stage of travel to the destination I had dreamed of visiting for so many years. Though the physical time could have been measured in minutes, as opposed to hours—it seemed to stretch on forever. I was able to truly center myself. This, even though the periodic pains in my stomach were a reminder of my humanness.

As we approached the gates of Bodh Gaya, the experience was similar to that of driving into the parking lot of *Disneyland*. It was somewhat like entering an amusement park—as sanctified as it may be. The gates, which held back the masses from this holy ground, were prominent. And, as is the case with much of India's holy sites, numerous individuals flanked the gates with their hands extended, requesting alms.

As we pulled up, the driver asked me for the necessary amount of money to pay the gatekeeper the entrance fee. I reached in pocket and supplied him with the appropriate Rupees.

As we begin to enter the sacred location, out from the group of beggars steps my Shama Baba. I immediately thought, *"I should have expected this."* *"Wait!"* I told the driver. He reluctantly stopped. I smiled at my friend as I opened the door of the Taxi.

"Hello, Baba," he stated, *"Not feeling too well?"* He continued, *"I've been waiting for you. What took you so long?"*

I scooted over in my seat and he got it. The driver was none too happy.

Like a child, Shama Baba entered the taxi—experiencing it as if it was one of the most illustrious things on the planet Earth. He sat down, looked around, wide-eyed.

I reached around him and closed his door. The driver gave me a rather dirty look and drove on. We continued our drive.

There is a very specific and highly regarded parking location for the taxis who have driven seemingly wealthy, spiritual travelers, like myself, who make the pilgrimage to Bodh Gaya. As there is virtually no way to hail a taxi if you don't keep yours in wait, the drivers get to hang out for as long as it takes for the Western travelers to transverse the ground while the meter is running. Well, there are actually no meters, but metaphorically speaking.

I was surprised; it was only about thirty feet to a parking spot. I didn't realize it would be so close or I would have gotten out instead of inviting Shama Baba in.

After a few moments of pause, as I studied Shama Baba's intrigue, I suggested that we get out.

Almost ignoring me, he was still wide eyes and continued studying every crevasse of the interior. I got out, walked around the car, and open the door for him. Finally, he joined me—eyes still fixed on the interior.

I did quite know which way to travel. I walked somewhat lackadaisically. As I did, while he was still looking back at the taxi, he pointed, *"That way."*

Bodh Gaya—there are an untold number of crumbling ancient stupa everywhere. They were not so massive as the ones in Angor Wat, Cambodia, or as distinctive as the stupas in Pagan, Burma, nor so adorned or flamboyant as the ones in Thailand. But, they did illustrate the centuries of worship this place has undergone.

We walked the grounds, entered the Buddha Museum, where the remains of age-old statues of Siddhartha Guatama were on display. We went to the site of the Bodhi Tree, where Buddha had found his enlightenment. *"Probably not the same tree,"* I thought. *"No tree could live that long."*

The overall feeling of Bodh Gaya was like that of a photograph of a young beautiful woman, who you fantasize about. But, when you final meet her, she is a hundred years old. All that was, is gone. All that remains is the memories of what used to be.

As we walked a *Sanyassin* was passing out *Pursad, "Blessed food."* His orange robes clearly defined him from the green and brown surroundings. Still very sick and not wishing to add fuel to the fire of my dysentery, I passed on the sacrament. Shama Baba smiled and took some. As he stuck it in his month, he motioned with his other hand that I give the man some money. I smiled, handed him a few

38

rupees, put my hands in prayer position and gave the man *pranam.*

Shama Baba walked on. A short distance from the *Sanyassin,* he said, *"They wear their titles like crowns for you to worship."*

Well now, there was a sharp blow. *"Aren't the holy men of India, holy,"* I mentally questioned?

Immediately, without my saying a word, he answered, as if he had read my thoughts.

"All these things are only things—this is this and that is that. But they only exist to feed your illusion. A Swami is not a Swami simply by the clothing he wears. A Buddha is not a Buddha simply because people write fantastic stories about him. He lived thousands of years ago and spoke pretty words. But, you cannot see him or touch him, how do you know he really lived?"

He paused, finished his *pursad,* licked his fingers and then continued,

"By being—the truth of all things is lost. Not being is Samadhi."

He looked at me as if to view my reaction. Then, he smiled,

"All things are as they are, Baba. Simply exist and everything you need will come to you." With a knowing glance, he looked deeply into my eyes and said, *"I think you already know this, Baba?"*

There was something very deep inside of me that did know that what he said was true. Immediately, he stated,

"You see, Baba, you do know."

He begins to walk away. I followed him attempting to absorb the depth of what he had said. We were approaching the gates of Bodh Gaya, he went on,

"You only need be here on vacation, Baba, there is nothing to seek in India—nothing to look for. You already have it all. Just be like Mata Ganga, she flows helping and nourishing who she can. If someone drinks her waters, she lets them drink. The Ganges does not call herself a goddess. It is man who worships her. She is only following her path down to the sea."

We were approaching my taxi. The driver, who was lying in the driver seat with his shirt off, wearing only a white tee shirt, jumped up and begins putting his shirt on.

"You should go back to Delhi now maybe you won't feel so sick." Then he laughed.

I was rather numb by the whole experience. The let-down of Bodh Gaya and the profound words this beggar, who had come out of nowhere, had imparted upon me.

Before I could think too much, he said,

"Oh, by the way, Baba, do you have any small money with you for the little girl so she can eat?"

He smiled and pointed to her patiently waiting with the other beggars who flanked the gates of Bodh Gaya. I reached into my pocket and gave him all the money I had. He began to walk away, turned, and said, *"Remember, Baba, never be scared, just flow like the Ganges into your own perfection."*

In somewhat of a daze of jet-lag: India, dysentery, and seeking the essence of spirituality, I made my way back to my hotel. I spend a few more days in Varanasi, bathing in *Mata Ganga* each day, and then headed back for Delhi. After I recuperated in Delhi for a week or so, I headed North, up to Rishikesh. There, I was guided down a completely different path of spirituality—one that appeared very holy but was not. It took me a couple of years to come to the understanding that those who appear to be spiritual are never the truly spiritual. It took me some more time to truly understand the spiritual simplicity of what Shama Baba had taught me. So simple, yet so true. I had to develop the ability to put away preconceived notions and to embrace true understanding.

The Essence of India

That is the essence of India. There is spirituality and spiritual teachers everywhere. There are also many illusions placed in the path of the seeker. If you think you can tell the difference, think again. Because, the *Maya, "Illusion,"* is very subtle. Some of us, who travel there, are lucky enough to be guided towards our own ultimate realization. But first, you must know who you are, what you are, why you are, and understand your own destiny. If not, you can be led down a very long road to nowhere.

Remember, however, ultimately, every road leads to enlightenment.

As I write these pages it has now been more than twenty years since I last saw Shama Baba. Though I have returned to India several times, I have never found him again. Perhaps that is the perfection of the true teacher, they give you all the knowledge you need, and then they turn and walk away...

If you every see him, tell him I said, *"Hi."*

Chapter 3
Surrender

Most people who enter onto *the Spiritual Path* are drawn to it very early in their life. The majority of these people don't take the steps to actualize their early instincts until they have lived through one too many traumas and are encountering a complete lack of meaning in their life. This explains why there are all the formally depicted reasons for, *"Becoming Spiritual,"* desperation, illness, poverty, loss of a loved one, and so on. Even in the cases when an individual is propelled into spirituality based in those negative motivating circumstances, if they were not touched by the divine early in life, they would not choose spirituality over the more destructive forms of mourning, such as drugs, alcoholism, sex addiction, and crime.

From a personal perspective, defined by whatever unexplained *Karma* or destiny, I formally entered onto what may be called, *"The Spiritual Path"* very early in my life. I was drawn to Eastern Mysticism as far back as I can remember. As I grew up, in the 1960's and 1970's, the terms: *Guru, Karma, Yoga, Zen, and Meditation* were commonplace, as were photos of Indian Spiritual Teachers gracing the walls of head shops, homes, billboards, and telephone poles. I suppose being born in Los Angeles, where this type of mindset was much more commonly embraced than in many other parts of the country, didn't hurt to aid in the availability of the spirituality that I came to heartily embrace and allow to formally shape the person I was to become.

Sixteen

When I was sixteen years old, a friend of mine came knocking at my door. I had not seen him in over a year.

We had met when he was a senior and I was a sophomore at *Hollywood High School.* During our preliminary friendship we realized that we were both drawn to *the Spiritual Path.* We would spend hours talking about the various philosophies and ideologies of Hinduism, Taoism, and Zen. But initially, we were not able to take the next step and move into the more refined realms of spirituality as neither of us had a car and we had no way to travel to spiritual centers where we could meet the teachers. This all changed a year later.

Post him showing up at my Hollywood apartment that evening, we both progressed into a period of rapid spiritual awakening. We would drive around with *Malas, "Prayer Beads,"* hanging from the rear-view mirrors of our cars, pictures of Krishna or images of the Buddha taped to our dash boards, listening to the music of Ravi Shankar and Bhagavan Das or lectures by Ram Dass and Alan Watts. As we drove, we would chant while the passenger played the bamboo flute. We spent the next year or so frequenting all of the spiritual centers along the West Coast. My friend eventually went off to college in Santa Cruz and I found *the Sufi Order* and Swami Satchidanada's, *Integral Yoga Institute.* Though I was intrinsically much more drawn to the joy that was brought about by the singing and dancing which served as a meditation tool to *the Sufi Order. None-the-less*, I found myself spending many nights practicing *Hatha Yoga* or lost deep in meditation with my new friends at the IYI.

As I look back, I realize how quickly I moved through the ranks of the IYI and quickly found myself in the inner circle of the group with direct access to Swami Satchidananda. This was in no small part due to the fact of my love for Rock n' Roll I had already acquired a vast knowledge about audio taping and how to operate sound systems. Thus, I became *Gurudev's* soundman—traveling to his lectures, doing his sound, and recording his talks for posterity.

Brahamcharya

It was at one such function in Santa Barbara, where *Yogaville West* was located at the time, that Swamiji had given a public talk. Though I was a practicing *Brahamcharya, "Celibate,"* and planned to be for the rest of my life, I had brought along this female friend of mine to meet Swamiji.

I had met her at *the Sufi Dances* and she and I were very attracted to one another. At the time, I believed that if anyone were worth giving up my lifelong plan of celibacy for, it would be her.

Post the lecture, which went exceedingly well, as I was always very conscientious and concerned about the sound being exact, *Gurudev* returned to his home in Montecito overlooking the Pacific Ocean, and the IYI inner circle gathered at a vegetarian restaurant in Chula Vista—the University town just North of Santa Barbara.

The gathering was coming to a close. It was my female friends and my plan to go camping in the Santa Monica Mountains that evening where our infatuation was leading towards consummation. She and I were preparing to leave when this female *Swami* came up to me and said, *"Shiva Dass, my ride has left, you must drive me back to L.A."*

Well, this put me in quite a quandary. I mean, it was getting late and to drive her back to the Hollywood IYI would kill all of the plans my friend and I had in place.

This *Swami* was a female born on the East Coast and though she had embraced *the Spiritual Path* she certainly maintained all of the abrupt inner-city traits commonly associated with the East Coast lifestyle. In other words, what she had said to me was not so much a question, but more like a command. I looked at my friend, she at me.

It was one of those moments that seem to go on for an eternity. In that seeming eternity, however, I truly embraced my inner being—that inside place where you simply know. I saw my physical persona, seriously infatuated with this girl, and then I witnessed my pure spiritual being—who knew that if I couldn't step outside of my own desires and help those who needed help, what did the spiritual life truly mean.

I surrendered; I was going to give her a ride home. In that moment of surrender, the *Swami's* missing ride, reappeared. She had not left, as was suspected. But, had simply gone off to the beach for a gaze at the setting sun. I was saved!

I sat there in the restaurant knowing that it was my surrender, to the situation, which caused Divananda to reappear. Had I fought the test I was given, then my drive down the coast would have included another passenger.

The party broke up with *Pranams, "Prayer Hands," to* everyone. My female friend and I were in my car heading South—off to the camping spot which she knew of.

By the time we arrived in the Santa Monica Mountains, it was quite dark. And, though we looked and looked, she could not find the camping location. It was decided to give up our adventure. I drove her home to her house in Bel Aire.

The Moral of the Story

We all have the tendency to plan. This episode is the perfect example of the unpredictability of life.

We each set our desires in place and expect them to be actualized. The problem is, there is no guarantee that anything we plan or hope for will come to volition. Not a physical desire, which defined this experience for me, not the enlightenment which is promised at some future date or lifetime to all of those who tread upon *the Spiritual Path*, not even the assurance that you will be physically alive to experience anything in the next moment.

With this understanding in place, the most spiritual thing you can do each moment of your physical existence, is to surrender to the fact that, *"All is unknown. Nothing is guaranteed."* You cannot know what your next experience will be. You can hope, you can desire, you can plan. But hope, desire, and planning are just that. They are what the definition of those words equal—something that is predicated upon expectation. Expectations remove you from the now. Expectations are as far from Zen as you can get.

Because Zen is only about the Here and the Now.

Surrender

What does it mean to surrender? Surrender is embracing the unknown. Surrender is accepting that nothing is promised.

Accepting that nothing is promised, you are allowed to encounter each moment in its perfection. Encountering each moment in its perfection is the essence of Zen.

Well, though the girl and I remained close for a time, we never had the opportunity to take our infatuation to the next level. She eventually became a Scientologist. Me, I went to India.

Surrender, because in that surrender all is allowed to be as it should be.

Chapter 4
Consciousness

Zen is a pathway of consciousness. The more consciously you live your life, the more direct your path towards spiritual realization.

Defining Consciousness

People on *the Spiritual Path* commonly talk about consciousness. But, what is consciousness? Many believe it to be some mystical state that can only be achieved by an ancient sage after years of meditation. This type of definition removes consciousness from the realms of the *here and now*. It makes it something distant and unobtainable and provides the framework for all kinds of justifications why you cannot become conscious, *Right Here, Right Now.*

As human beings, schooled by this modern world, we have, in fact, been guided away from consciousness. There are an untold number of distractions, self-orientated philosophies, and teachers who guide us towards selfishness, but not consciousness.

Consciousness must, therefore, be redeveloped by each of us. This is accomplished by transcending the limitations of learned physical existence and evolving to a new level of universal awareness and understanding.

The Bathroom Detail

When I was sixteen or seventeen, I was asked to accompany a fellow disciple, a professional electrician, whose spiritual name was Bhagwan, to the Montecito home of our *Guru,* Swami Satchidananda. I was to assist in the installation of our *Guru's* jacuzzi. Though I had spent a lot of time in the presence of my *Guru,* I had not been invited to his home. So, I was obviously filled with an untold amount of youthful exuberance.

Bhagwan and I arrived early in the morning and spent the day working on the jacuzzi. Occasionally *Swamiji* would come out, check on our progress, correct the logistical mistakes he thought Bhagwan had made, and occasionally make joke with me or pat me on the head. He was obviously amused that I was much younger than the majority of his disciple. I was still in High School...

This personalized interaction was, of course, a higher honor than I could ever have hoped for at that point in my life.

As the day concluded, we were scheduled to travel a few miles up the coast to *Yogaville West,* were *Swamiji* was to give a talk to his disciples. As we were a bit dirty, our *Guru* invited us to use his personal bathroom to clean up. This was a blessing of an unparalleled degree. When I later related this fact to the other disciples, their jaws all dropped in disbelief that we were allowed to use the *Guru's* bathroom.

Bhagwan was the first in. He took seemingly forever. I sat on *Gurudev's* bed, anxiously waiting, knowing that Bhagwan was taking way too long. When I finally was allowed in, the bathroom was a mess. Bhagwan had left dirty water all over the sink; the dirty towels he had whipped his hands with were thrown haphazardly on the ground. I couldn't believe it! I immediately got to work cleaning up his mess. Approximately two minutes into the job, a knock came upon the door and *Swamji's* secretary said I really needed to hurry up, as *Gurudev* needed to get ready. So, I had only a moment or two to finish my clean-up of Bhagwan's mess and to wash my own hands.

I exited none too happy with my spiritual brother. I mean, how could he do that? Make a mess and leave it for me to clean up. And, he made me look I was the one taking way too long...

I was very young and naive, so I keep my opinions to myself, as he was in his early thirties with a family and a job. But even then, I understood conscious verse unconscious actions.

Not to be critical of any individual, but we all possess our own set of foundations. Me, I was taught that you should not make a mess in someone else's house. Bhagwan, even though he possessed the outward appearance of walking *the Spiritual Path*, obviously had not learned the same lesson—nor had he opened himself up to the level of consciousness where you take other people into consideration.

The First Step to Consciousness

You must begin at the beginning. The first step on your path of consciousness begins with your foundations—with what you already know.

You must study yourself and detail how you have learned to act and react to situations. For example, what would you have done if you found yourself in the aforementioned situation? How would you have naturally reacted?

Once you have defined these areas of your personality, you must consciously decide if they are right or if they are wrong.

Each of us will find areas that appear to be fine and other areas where we know we need to change. This is the point where you make your first conscious decision to make the person you are into the more universally conscious person you hope to become.

This is not necessarily easy. For we have all learned how to react certain ways—encounter specific situations with a particular attitude and interact with people in a prescribed manner. For the most part, this education never took place in a formal manner. We, as children and young adults, learn how to treat people and encounter situations from those around us. In many cases, we learned from people whose lifestyles were in complete contrast to consciousness. Thus, you must focus and motivate your own change.

Change does not occur overnight. It must be practiced.

This is where your first formalized steps into consciousness take place. You must decide to alter an area of your own personality and then do it.

If you slip and retreat to your old patterns of behavior, don't beat yourself up about it. Simply realize that you are on *the Spiritual Path*. *The Spiritual Path* is a *step-by-step* road to realization. You are now taking the initial steps you need to becoming the more conscious individual you know will emerge.

Keep in mind, that this preliminary step to consciousness is essentially important. For without a complete internal assessment, you can never hope to truly know yourself. You will simply pass through life reacting unconsciously to whatever situation you may encounter. This is the most animalistic level of human evolution.

Without knowing self, you can never transcend self. Transcendence requires that you know where you are ascending from and what you are ascending to. Thus, knowing YOU, is the first step of refined consciousness.

R. Buckminster Fuller

When I was a university undergraduate, I observed another interesting occurrence, which delineated varying levels of consciousness. R. Buckminster Fuller, one of the greatest analytical minds of the twentieth century, came to speak at my campus. The hall was stuffed beyond capacity, and they were not allowing anyone else to enter. I was not willing to be turned away, however, so I eventually found my way up to the second level mezzanine where the spotlights found their source. From there, I could see and hear him fine.

He began his talk at about 12:30. A little before 1:00, half of the audience began to get up and leave. He asked, *"Where are you going?"* *"To class,"* was the answer, which rang from the mobile audience. *"Why are you going to class?"* Bucky exclaimed. *"They have nothing to teach you. But, I do!"* Unfazed, the exodus continued.

I was standing there in disbelief—nobody even knew what Bucky was about. He was just a name and a lecture to attend during lunch.

For me, this optimized the perfect example of unfocused consciousness. You do something for the doing, with no mental content.

The lecture proceeded with half of the auditorium empty.

The Second Step to Consciousness

The second step to consciousness is to consciously perform all actions.

To focus your consciousness, you must make all of your actions as precise as possible. This is how all of the great spiritual teachers have truly given something to this world.

As long as you do not think or do not care, your acts will forever remain simply unconscious actions. Unconscious actions only cause reactions.

If you wish your acts to transcend the limitations of this material world, you must do whatever it is you do from a perspective of pure one-pointed consciousness.

Doing things conscious is not as easy as it may sound. For example, think about the brown rice you prepare. When you wash your rice before you cook it, do you ever allow a few grains to fall into the sink and be swept away? If so, think about this next time you are hungry. How many of those grains of rice, that you have unconsciously let slip away, would it take to fill your stomach?

This is obviously simply an example. But, if you wish to enter the realms of true consciousness you must do everything you do in a very refined manner.

There will always be mental justifications to forgive yourself for the unconscious actions you take if you allow yourself to accept them. If, on the other hand, you choose to live a life of consciousness, those justifications can never be embraced.

The Third Step to Consciousness

The next step in ascending consciousness is you must ask yourself, *"What are you doing with your life?"* If you cannot answer that question, you are not walking the path of consciousness. Thus, you must take the time to sit down and define what is going on around you. Formally designate what has taken place in your life and what has led you to where you are today.

The best way to do this is to actually write it down so it is in front of you in black and white and can be studied. From this, you will gain perspective. From perspective you can conclude how you have ended up where you have ended up. Thus, you can chart the next step in your life from a place of consciousness.

Once the first question is answered, you must then ask yourself, *"Why you are doing what you are doing?"* Because without formulated reasoning, what you are doing is simple what you are doing. It is not performed consciously.

Nobody can tell you why you are doing what you are doing. Not religion, not astrology, not your loved ones. You are you. Each person is based in a secular consciousness. You have lived what you have live. These factors have defined the person you have become. Before you can transcend the limitations of self, you must know who self is.

So, at this point, acutely detail why you are doing what you are doing. You may like what you find. If so, then nothing needs changing. If not, then you must be the one to consciously make that change.

The biggest mistake that people commonly make at this stage of life analysis is that they decide they hate their job, hate their mate, hate their life and they throw it all to the wind. This is not consciousness.

From a perspective of consciousness, you make changes to your life consciously. You chart out your actions, how they will affect others, and then you move towards a desired end in a slow controlled manner. From this, you do not damage the lives of others, nor do you leave yourself destitute.

The Forth Step to Consciousness

This is the stage where you begin to formalize your Spiritual Pathway. Though you have no doubt been walking *The Spiritual Path* throughout each of the previous stages, at this point you formally make it the defining element to your life.

Many people believe to do this that they must leave the material world behind and move to an *ashram* or go to India, Nepal, Thailand, or Japan. This is incorrect.

Going is only going. Though you may have new experiences, you may even have fun, going is not the pathway to consciousness, as going is based in desire.

In Zen, we understand that everything you need to find spiritual enlightenment is *Right Here, Right Now.* Going only takes you away from the here and the now. Thus, going never leads to *Nirvana.*

To become consciously spiritual, is to accept.

Life is life and there will be trials and tribulations. Many people falsely believe that they should not happen to a spiritual person. Yet, they do.

Embracing truly conscious spirituality is about accepting the perfection. Knowing that all is as it should be. If you want things to be different you are only embracing a mindset bound by desire.

The consciously spiritual person understands that by letting go of desires, they will be joyous at any life occurrence, as they will see it as a pathway to further refinement of consciousness.

Consciousness Unconsciousness

There are some people who walk the path of spirituality and place reasoning behind their unconsciousness. They provided seemingly poetic statement to justify their unconscious actions. *"I am just doing what I am doing. I am simply a leave which has enter the stream of life and am flowing as nature guides me."*

Yes, you can place a leave in the stream and, yes, it will flow until it reaches the ocean or is stopped by some obstacle. But, does it care that it is flowing in the stream? No, it does not. It is simply flowing the path that was laid out before it, with lack of consciousness.

To consciously enter the stream of life is very different from unconsciously ending up in the stream of life and ending up wherever it is you end up. This is why you must take control and refine your consciousness.

The refinement of consciousness can only begin with you. Ultimately, consciousness is how you interact with this place we call life. Consciousness is the thoughts you think, leading to the actions you take. Consciousness is what you do and how you do it. Consciousness is your choice.

Choose to live consciously and Nirvana becomes obvious.

Chapter 5
Energy and the Spiritual Path

It is a very common experience to meet an individual or enter into a confined atmosphere and encounter an overpowering sense of a very specific type of energy. Most commonly, the two types of energy, that is noticeably experienced, are a powerful negative force or a very peaceful energy. The reason that these two forms of energy are readily noticed is that we, as human being, have wholly experienced these energies and in some cases come to embrace one of these two highly differing forces, allowing it to define our lives.

Yin and Yang

Negativity is a dark force. It is the *Yang* energy of the universe. Peace is the light force, the *Yin* element of life.

As has been defined for thousands of years, these two highly differing energies make up all of human existence. When one or the other of these forces is heartily embraced, the energy of a specific individual is permeated with this essence. When one specific type of energy is embraced over a long period of time it expands from the individual or group and comes to be locked into any object, or surrounding environment. Thus, saturating the location with a very specific type of energy.

The first time that an energy force noticeably overpowered me was when I was fourteen years old and two men who lived in my apartment building in Hollywood, California asked me to help them move.

We made numerous trips up and down the stairs, loading their possessions into the back of a U-Haul trailer. One of the last items remaining in their bedroom was a small black branch, which was leaning against the wall. Being youthful and thinking nothing of it, I picked it up and was immediately overpowered by the sheer force of dark and evil energy. I immediately placed it back on the floor. But, my hand remained tingling from its power.

Later, one of the men explained that it was the black magic wand of his partner. He continued that this man had been involved in devil worship previous to their relationship. This obviously explained why the branch was so powerfully impacted with dark energy.

The next time I encountered a force of energy was thankfully emanating from a much purer source. I was a young man on my way to India for the first time. En route, I stopped off in Hong Kong for a few days and had taken the hydrofoil to Macau. With no real destination in mind, I simply walked. I found myself atop this hill, where there was located a Christian shrine devoted to the Mother Mary. The moment I entered the area, the peace and tranquility that emanated from this location was intense. I was overwhelmed by the profound calmness, which I encountered. I sat for a long time, simply embracing this tranquility, wondering how this outdoor sanctuary, in the middle of Southeast Asia, had become so permeated with this divine essence.

The next time I encountered a very powerful form of energy was when I was walking the busy streets of Bangkok, Thailand a few years later. As I followed the sidewalk, approaching me from the opposite direction was a lady approximately forty years old. My eyes could not look away from her. As she got closer, the power of evil, which permeated from her being, was overwhelming. So much so that as we passed, her eyes fixed upon me, and I felt like I was going to pass out. It took all of my meditative focus to remain centered and continue walking away from her negative presence.

People: Dark and Light
The overtly negative or dark individual is commonly going to attempt to force their energy upon you. This is due to the fact that dark energy, no matter what its source, be it based in a religion or simply the desire to overpower another human being, is an obtrusive energy—it permeates from a source and seeks to overpower and destroy.

The individual, who is highly embraced by peaceful energy, seeks to control, convert, or overpower no one. Thus, simply being in their presence is enough to make you more peaceful.

These are just a few of the more extreme example of the power of energy when it is acutely focused. For the most part, the average individual does not possess enough mental focus to define their energy, be it positive or negative, in such a dramatic fashion. Most people pass through life oblivious to the type of energy, which they are focusing upon and emulating. This, however, is where the real problems begin. Because when a person is not conscious of what energy surrounds them, they are not only unknowingly dominated by it but are projecting it to all those whom they encounter.

The other side of the coin is there are those people who believe that they have the power to toy with a specific type of energy, once they have defined its source. The problem is, though these individuals may be aware of the type of energy they are encountering, they have not developed the necessary skills to combat its force.

The Dark Path

I have a friend who knows this man who used to worship the devil. First of all, it is important to clarify that the worship of any negative energy can only breed negativity. Whether or not you believe the superstitions portrayed in works such as the Bible or the untold number of literary works, movies, and television episodes that have given credence to this style of mythology is unimportant. Energy is energy and the focusing upon the negative only brings that style of energy more clearly into physical presence.

My friend, the moment things would be going well for him, would say, *"Let's test it."* At which point he would invite the man back into his life and inevitably things would go wrong.

The reasoning for this is twofold. One, negative energy is very powerful, and it easily overpowers the untrained mind, body, and spirit, of the unequipped. Secondarily, by inviting negative energy in, you have already submitted to its power. Thereby, you will lose any confrontation to it, whether physical or spiritual.

It is like the old adage, *"The devil cannot enter unless he is invited in."* This is an important thing to remember when dealing with the various levels of energy you will encounter on *the Spiritual Path*. As long as you remain positive, positivity will find you. The moment you embrace the negative, it will be very difficult to free yourself from its alluring power.

Why then, you may ask, does a person ever desire to become involved with negative energy? First of all, it is empowering. The type of individual who seeks out the source of this energy, in the forms of religion, personal associations, or physical items which they surround themselves with such as art objects and trinkets, are generally those who have had less than an idealistic life. Thus, the power of evil promises solace for those who have not found fulfillment in the more savory aspects of life.

Certainly, this is a simplified answer to a complex question. And, there are an untold number of events and motivations, which cause an individual to follow the path of negativity. But, it is essential to remember—energy attracts energy. Surround yourself with any specifically focalized form of energy and it will come to define your life.

The Power of Power

There is another style of much more subtle energy employed by the person who, for whatever self-determined logic, claims to be a spiritual teacher. An example of this is the case of a woman who I was introduced to by a friend a few years ago. She was a very pretty Asian lady in her mid-thirties. In the minds of many people, simply by being of Asian descent somehow instantly solidified that an individual must be spiritual. In any case, she was one of those individuals who had been exposed to the understanding of controlling the energy of another person.

It must be stated, in India for example, this style of energy manipulation is considered kindergarten on *the Spiritual Path*. When a *Yogi* progresses through the first stages of meditative understanding, it becomes relatively easy to master the *Siddha, "Spiritual Power,"* of manipulating and controlling the energy of another human being. The advancing *Yogi* understands, however, if you control someone else's energy, no matter what your motivation, you are taking on that person's *karma*. Thus, it is not the path to self-realization and is only practiced by the unenlightened.

The problem is, when certain individuals come to learn how easy it is to control the energy of another person, especially when a person is receptive to this control, which is commonly the case of those at the beginning stages of *The Spiritual Path*, they become lost in the power of this energy manipulation. Many of the people who develop this ability forgo any true spiritual inkling that they initially possessed and fall into the illusion of believing that they are a true spiritual teacher. They are not.

True spiritual teachers never attempt to alter the energy of another individual, for they understand that the road to realization is an individual pathway. They may give guidance, but they do not fall into the ego-based motivation of cultivating disciples by the use of their ability to alter the momentary reality of any person.

In the case of this woman, my friend was deeply in awe of her apparent spiritual powers. Knowing my involvement in spirituality, he insisted that I meet her. Which I happily agreed to do.

The day of the meeting occurred. She walked into the room, wearing expensive designer clothing. She had long black hair with bells hanging from the ends of her locks. She wore expensive jewelry and was adorned with an enormous amount of makeup. She smelled of expensive French perfume. I smiled...

From the description my friend had given me, I expected to meet a being of power. What I saw was an individual lost to the manifestations of the material world.

As she was politely on the quest for new disciples, she spoke to me. We discussed her path. She detailed how she began having visions of angels when she was very young and how she could channel their power to those who meditated at her feet. Her method for this channeling was the age-old technique of having disciples sit in front of her with the lights turned down low. Then, they would focus their gaze upon her form and were not to allowed to blink. Not to be unkind, but if you stare at anyone, without blinking, under those low light conditions, you will see all kinds of images.

As we spoke, I continued to experience her psychic power attempting to pierce the veil of my consciousness. Having long walked this path, and having met this style of teacher before, she was not successful.

The meeting eventually came to an end. She left and my friend expecting me to be as in awe of her as he was—he asked me what I thought. I answered, *"Does the Dalai Lama, wear perfume and makeup?"*

Perhaps the most interesting occurrence of this meeting was upon her exit; I attempted to use my cellular phone. The battery had gone dead and it would never take a charge again. The more cynical individual would simply chalk this up as a coincidence. I knew better.

There are many people out there who come to master some of the subtle energies of this universe. Some of these people use this mastery to positive ends. Some, on the other hand, use this power for negative goals. And, some simply thrive on the energy that they can extract from others. No matter what the ideology, the truly spiritual person exists only within his or her own perfection. They never attempt to draw upon, alter, or channel the energy of another person.

If you are trying to help someone by healing him or her, you take on their *karma*. By attempting to feed off of someone's energy, at any level, you are also taking on his or her *karma*. Thus, to interact consciously with universal energy, you must first purify your mind and spirit to the degree that your own personal wants or desires never enter into your action.

If you want someone to heal, you are existing in a place of desire. If you want someone who is sad to be happy, you are existing in a place of desire. If you want to be more invigorated, you are existing in a place of desire. If you think you are a teacher and you want people to follow you, you are existing in a place of desire. Desire is never the pathway to enlightenment.

Soon after the meeting, my friend was told by his spiritual teacher that I was a bad influence and that he should not associate with me any longer, as I did not see her as the True Teacher. So, we parted ways for a time until he ran out of money and could no longer afford to provide his *Guru* with the appropriate amount of financial support expected for her meditation sessions.

As he looks back now, older and wiser, he realizes that by opening himself up to her powers, she was allowed to hypnotism him to the degree that he would often times see and experience things which she would simply tell him were there. When, in fact, they were not.

This is the paradox of *The Spiritual Path*. People naturally seek guidance. When you seek guidance, guidance is readily found. The problem is, as the old saying goes, *"There is a sucker born every minute."* In the case of spiritual teachers, especially those who possess some low-level powers, their guidance is not the style of teaching that should be followed. As spiritual teaching based in undeserving reverence for the unenlightened individual only leads you down a path to inevitable destruction.

Energy is energy and through refined techniques you can come to consciously control it. Control is not the way of nature. Control only leads to your own inevitable loss. Throughout history we see that the powerful person, nation, or organization always falls due to the fact that power is temporal— the more you possess, the more you are guided away from the path of the naturally spiritual.

Power corrupts. Possess no power and you are free to be enlightened.

The Pyramids

Speaking of energy... There has been an enormous amount of historic, archaeological, and New Age literature written about the power of the Egyptian pyramids. So, the first time I traveled to Cairo I truly expected to encounter a lot of very powerful energy from these ancient structures.

My flight from Istanbul arrived in Cairo late in the afternoon. While waiting for a Taxi, which can take hours at the Cairo airport, I met these two exchange students who only had one night in the city before they went back to the States. So, they had to see to pyramids right away.

We shared a taxi. By the time we got to my *Five-Star* hotel, it was already dark. But, they were committed to going. So, we dropped off our luggage in my room and off we went. We grabbed a bus and made it to the site. In the darkness, the image of the pyramids is quite astounding.

As soon as we approached the site, we were accosted by a young man, early twenties, who wanted to take us on a camel back tour of the pyramids. For a price, of course. Though I am against riding animals, the two girls were up for it. So, more to watch over them, than anything else, I went along.

We rode around the pyramids to little avail. Nice, but...

After our ride, the man insisted that we come to his nearby house for tea. As an inner-city kid, I questioned his motives. But, the girls wanted to go. So again, to watch over them, I went along.

We entered the man's rustic home. Similar in style and structure to many in Cairo—the animals lived downstairs. The home was upstairs. Immediately upon entering, I noticed three other adult males. I didn't like what I was seeing. The girls, from the Midwest, did not take notice of the impending situation.

We were offered tea. I, of course, declined. The girls did not. Soon, as I would have predicted, they were feeling very sleepy and nodding out. They had been drugged...

I am not going to go into the whole story, but with a little quick-handed *bravado,* my years of martial arts training, etc., I got the girls out of there. They eventually walked off their imposed sleepiness. And, the next morning, I saw them off. I never heard from them again.

The moral of the story—just because you are in a seemingly holy or energy filled location, do not expect all of those who share the location with you to possess a similar mindset.

The Daytime Pyramids

After my newfound friends boarded a taxi the next morning for the airport, I got on a city bus and moved back towards these antediluvian structures.

After walking in their presence for several hours, and then climbing up their sides, (this was back when you could still do that), to become accustomed to the type of energy they expounded, I entered the passageway of *The Great Pyramid* and walked the upward pathway, hunched over, for a seeming eternity to enter *The King's Chamber*. With each step that I took I remained very conscious, attempting to allow the ancient energy of this pyramid to touch me. Finally, I arrived in *The King's Chamber. I* was completely alone. There was no one else willing to make the ascending journey to this core center of the pyramid. I stood there amazed that I was not experiencing anything. I sat down, quieted my mind, and meditated. Still, there was no experience of the acceding energy the pyramids are reported to provide. After sitting solo in *The King's Chamber* for several hours, I left.

It was my conclusion at the time, that whatever energy the pyramids once held had been lost or stolen long ago by the grave robbers and the archaeologists who looted these mighty tombs of their riches and antiquities. It was not until years later that a friend of mine said something very profound. She stated, *"The pyramids are just cemeteries."*

To the individual who holds a fascination with these ancient structures, it may almost be a sacrilege to hear such as statement. But, the innocence of those words hit me with a profound truth.

The pyramids were created as a shrine to dead kings and their close devotees. They were constructed with no care for the lives of the slaves who actually made them. In fact, there was complete disregard for the lives of the builders of these grand structures. No matter how much mythical reverence you wish to give to them—this is fact. Though they are beautiful constructs, they can only be associated with death—not life. As such, any energy that they may possess is only surrounded by human demise, not human life.

It is important to keep the source of energy in mind before you give yourself up to the pursuit of interaction with a specific energy. For though structures such as the pyramids are great architectural masterpieces, their essence is not about life force. Thus, seeking the energy of the pyramids is not a path to vitality and rejuvenation. It is just the opposite.

The Source of Energy

Energy comes in many forms and from many sources. It is not solely based in an individual's choice of worship. Energy emanates from you at all times. When this energy is allowed to flow from your body and mind in an unrefined, unharnessed fashion it can become evident in amusing ways. For example, one of the first times I noticed how individual energy can permeate an atmosphere occurred when I was in graduate school—living in a small apartment in Manhattan Beach, California. It was late at night, and I was struggling at the typewriter to get a long-written assignment completed, which was due the next day. The pressure was on and I was assuredly emanating all of the chaotic energy that goes *hand-in-hand* with acute stress.

The windows were closed in the apartment, as it was a cool winter night. So, my energy, as dissident as it was, became confined and harnessed.

A little bit after 2:00 A.M., as I continued to battle my way through the writing discourse, a painting which was hanging from my wall, out of nowhere, fell to the ground. There had been absolutely no earthquake or other physically jarring experiences—only the disorder of my energy. Immediately, I realized how the chaotic energy emanating from my being had caused it to fall.

This type of event is not uncommon. I have a friend who lives with a female roommate. She is one of those great souls who is a beautiful person but due to childhood trauma, suffered in the outback of Australia, she has been left with a lot of chaos in her life. She works from home; thus, her energy is commonly confined with no outlet. My friend often speaks of the strange occurrences which take place in his house: glasses falling from the shelves, pictures falling from the walls, and so on. He wondered was his place haunted. *"No,"* I told him, *"Just energized."* My advice was to open the windows, let some new life in to dissipate the confined energy.

Opening

"Opening," is a very important thing to do in your life as you walk *the Spiritual Path*. Not only should the windows of your home be opened—allowing new, non-stagnant, energy to enter but you should refresh your body and mind with new energy, as well.

Energy becomes very stagnant when it is trapped in any location. This is why when you enter the home of many elderly people the smell is much the same and the immediate feeling of energy blockage comes over you.

Certainly, this is not meant to cast any negative stereotypes upon the elderly. But, what commonly occurs, as a person gets older is that they get more and more set in their ways. Years before they have decided what they like and what they do not like. So, their homes are linked with objects that they came into possession of many years before. As the objects have defined a lifestyle and a person, they have not been exposed to any new circulation of energy in a long time. Thus, the energy surrounding the home is stagnant, locked, trapped, and has had no new influx for a generally long period.

The trapping of energy is not only assigned to the elderly. People do it all the time. They pack souvenirs, cherished objects, old clothing, and musical instruments that were played in childhood into boxed which are then placed in garages, attics, or storage units. Though the possessions are remembered and kept for sentimental reason, they are not allowed to breathe. Thus, their energy becomes trapped and stagnates.

It is very important that you do not let this type of energy stagnations happen in your life. For if you own something, and if its energy is trapped, it will only serve as a means of unwitting negative control over your life that will cause you to be unnecessarily burdened. Being unnecessarily burdened, you cannot rapidly move through the various levels of consciousness onto the ultimate goal of *Nirvana*.

For the logic of being bound by nothing, *Sadhus* and monks renounce all material possession. Owning nothing, they are controlled by nothing. Thus, they can forgo attachments to objects that actually have little meaning and live in a space of refined energy.

Let Go

Letting go is the key to a life undefined by nonspecific energy. If you use an object—keep it. In use, the energy of the object will be continually refreshed.

If you do not use an object—let it go. Give it away. Someone else may be able to put it into functional use so the energy of the universe can remain flowing, with minimal stagnation.

In your own life it is also essential that you allow the positive energy of nature to cleanse you. Do not simply go from work to the gym, to home, to sleep, to work again. Allow yourself to become free, like you were as a child or a young adult. Let the simple movements of nature cleanse and nourish your physical and spiritual being.

When it is a windy day—take a walk. Experience how the wind is blowing through your hair and your clothing. Mentally experience it refreshing your body, mind, and spirit, with new-invigorated natural energy.

On a rainy day, go outside. Leave your umbrella at home. Take a walk. *Get Wet!* As the raindrops hit you, feel them cleansing your soul—washing away any anger or negativity you possess. Allow the raindrops to purify your being from any negative energy that may be plaguing your life, focused at you from another person. Let the rain free you.

If it's a sunny day, go outside. Close your eyes, look up at the sun. Allow its purifying warmth and positive, life-giving energy, to permeate your entire being. Leaving you filled with a sense of power and a source point for positive spiritual expansion.

Remember when you were a child—how free you felt when you were on a swing. Go to the park. Go climb on a swing. Let go of that the fact that other adults or children may be looking at you. Who cares! *Swing...* With each upward movement, release all of the tension and anguish of your life. With each back swing, feel the power you possess over your life. Yes, you can do anything. Let the freedom, once commonly embraced as a child, come to permeate your entire being.

Zazen does not only occur in the Full Lotus Posture.

Energy is a Choice

Energy is your choice. By remaining stagnant, your energy dissipates until it exists no more. Meditation, though obviously beneficial to *the Spiritual Path*, only locks energy into your physical being. Though you can obviously emanate it in a much more refined manner once your meditations have become acutely focused, energy emanating from any singular being or organized group only becomes an expounding of internalized and personalized energy.

Never become so vain that you believe that you have refined energy to the degree that you should pass your energy onto another individual. Each person has his or her own life to live and you have yours to live. Just like putting the wrong blood type into an injured victim, by attempting to focus your energy on any person and empower them with it, you are only giving them an energy that you think they need. Your energy may be very toxic to them, however.

Allow the energies you encounter in the world to pass through you. Do not attempt to hide from them. If they are negative, simply reflect them like a mirror. Do not attempt to harness them. If they are positive, let them enter you, nourish you, and then flow onwards.

Life is life and as was defined in ancient India, *Prana, "Universal Life Energy"* is everywhere and is constant. Let this understanding of energy embrace you and fill you with enhanced energy when it is needed. But, never attempt to possess and own *Prana* for then you only cause blockage and resistant to the natural flow of Universal Energy.

As we learn from the first law of thermodynamics, *"No energy in this universe can be created or destroyed."* Let energy touch, then flow to the next source where it is needed.

Universal Energy is free. You too should be free. Open your windows, move your body, embrace nature and you will become constantly full of positive, life fulfilling energy.

Energy begins with you.

Chapter 6
Where Myths Are Born

One evening, a number of years ago, I walked into *the Bodhi Tree Bookstore* on Melrose Avenue in West Hollywood, California. This bookstore has been a favorite haunt for us spiritual types for decades, because it is not only one of the first, but still one of the best bookstores catering to the spiritual lifestyle in the U.S.

As I walked down the aisles this particular evening, I noticed a book of stories. It was written by disciples about my one-time spiritual teacher Swami Satchidananda. I was obviously curious.

I picked up the book and flipped through the pages. As I did, I was drawn to the story of how, on this one warm Autumn afternoon, at a beach side home in Santa Barbara, California, *Gurudev,* as we called him, decided to go surfing. The story went on to describe that though this was the first time he had attempted the sport, once he was in the water, he paddled into a wave, and was standing up surfing like a pro.

As I read the words, I was both amazed and saddened by the tale that was being told. The individual who wrote the story was creating this amazing incident. Though amazing, it was a virtual impossibility, as can be attested to by anyone who can remember the first time they attempted to mount a surfboard. But, more than that, and what truly hurt me and caused me to come to a new realization about the truth of tales told to the masses is that this depiction was not at all what truly occurred.

The Two Surfers

There were two avid surfers among Swami Satchidananda's close disciples at that period of time. One was a carpenter named Ram Dass (not the famous Ram Dass) and the other was myself.

On the fateful day, detailed in the story, there was a get together of a small group of close disciples at the aforementioned Santa Barbara home of a new devotee. As there was a surfboard leaning against the house, *Gurudev* decided to give it a try. He asked Ram Dass and myself to help. In pure devotional fashion we were happy to do so.

We cautiously walked *Gurudev* out to where the water was approximately waist deep. This was because of the fact that Swami Satchidananda was well into his sixties at this point in time. At this juncture, we helped *Gurudev* climb onto the surfboard. We then swam him out a bit further to where the waves were breaking. He held on as we turned the surfboard around. We waited for a wave and then we pushed him into it. Laying on his stomach and holding fast onto the surfboard, he glided in towards the shore. We swam after him.

Did he stand up? No. Did he ride the surfboard like a pro? No. Did he want to try it again? No. Did he have fun? I think so.

Yet, in the story told in the book, he had instantly stood up, as his hair and his beard were blowing in the wind. He was a master surfer.

Exaggeration

Reading this story made me realize something very important. For some reason, people always want to exaggerate the life and actions of the spiritual teacher. They want to take mere mortal occurrences and blow them up to exaggerated proportions. Why? I don't know. Is it simply to make the *Guru* seem Godlike? Or, is it that this is how the devotional mind of an individual causes them to witness the occurrences?

For example, was the person who wrote this story, (and I remember her well), so spiritually in love with Swami Satchidananda that her mind took reality and transformed it into a new state of grace? Again, I don't know her motivation for changing fact to fiction.

What I do know is how this event actually occurred—for better or worse.

More than simply an individual relating their perceptions of this event, is the fact that an untold number of people have read this story in the book and believed it to be true.

It is published in a book, it must be true— right?

I believe this is an important lesson that we all must learn when we look to the lives of spiritual teachers—from the most unknown to supreme beings like Jesus and Buddha. For the most part, none of us were there to witness the immaculate events that are said to have been performed by the various spiritual teachers. Yet, their actions have been depicted in an untold number of works of literature throughout time. Whether these events actually occurred or not can only be known by those who were there. Yet, as we have seen, these events can be altered. Thus, what is written is not always true.

What can we conclude from all of this? Well, my conclusion is that, what difference does it make if a teacher can perform miracles. The miracle of yesterday is simply the magic trick of today, and the scientific proof of tomorrow.

Spirituality is beyond action. Action is defined by the realms of the material world. Inaction is the only true spirituality. So, if it doesn't matter what you can do, why should anybody care about what you can't do?

THINK ZEN...

Chapter 7
On the Inside Looking Out

When one thinks about those who walk upon *the Spiritual Path*, the idealized image of an individual wearing long robes, with a shaven head, or a *Sadhu* with long dreadlocked hair and a long beard is commonly the first thoughts that comes to mind. These external images of apparent holiness are etched onto the minds of the masses. This provides the average individual with a basis for the belief that one is not truly holy if they wear normal clothing and have a job to go to. But, this is very far from the truth.

Ram Dass

When I was an adolescent, forging my way on *the Spiritual Path*, I sent a letter to the modern American *Guru,* Ram Dass. I posed him a few questions, which my adolescence mind believed to be very important at the time. Though I was not sure that someone so seemingly holy as Ram Dass would have the time to answer, a month or so later, a reply did arrive in the mail. Yes, a letter from the man himself. As I read his hand-written words, I found that he had not only answered my questions, but also personally invited me to meet with him at a gathering he had scheduled in Los Angeles the following month. My youthful mind was awh struck.

The day of the gathering arrived, and I made my way to the location. I walked into the room and there he was, Baba Ram Dass. The man who the spiritual media had made mythical.

As he came up to greet me, I was somewhat set back, however. He wore a pull over sweater and a pair of drawstring pants. Somehow, I had expected him to be wearing the traditional clothing of a *Yogi,* a *dhoti* and a *kurta.* I mean, all of my friends on *The Spiritual Path*, and myself, wore pseudo *Yogi* clothing. Why didn't he?

This erroneous mindset is the perfect example of what is possessed by many individuals of this modern era. Holiness is gauged by external appearance. It is for this reason that so many people play, *"Dress up."* They somehow believe that if they wear the robes of a monk, have the dreadlocks of a *Sadhu,* they will be holy. But, this is all folly.

The Young Swami

There is an amusing story that details the other side of this issue and views how an individual who is not walking upon *The Spiritual Path* perceives one who is.

When I was in my third semester of college, I had already long been living the spiritual lifestyle. As such, I had been initiated into the *Order of Sannyas* and was wearing the orange clothing that delineated my standing.

My collegian friends would just call me, *"Swami"* or *"Monk,"* as most of them couldn't get their tongues around the longer version of the spiritual name I had been given. They were all very supportive of my path, however, commonly asking questions.

I was taking a class on philosophy—which at that time was my major. The instructor was an aging professor. He was one of those people who projected the mindset that he knew everything and the students knew nothing.

We took our midterms. Though academic Philosophy is about as far from the root source of the word as one can get, *none-the-less*, I believed I had done okay.

When the tests were returned the following class meeting, I was presented with the grade of, *"F."* Down the side of my paper was a long discourse on why I had received the grade. *"You cannot be a Swami, you are too young. You do not know enough. You will never know enough. You are Caucasian, not East India, etc., etc., etc..."* There was, however, no comment about my actual essay answers.

At the time, this professor's attitude shook me. Having surrounded myself, from a young age, with those walking upon *The Spiritual Path* or those friends who were accepting, I had never encountered this style of prejudice.

The grade I received made my classmates quite angry—much more angry than it made me. I was of the belief, *"It all is as it is. It is all perfection..."*

When I left the class that day, I wondered how I was even going to pass the course if I was to be judge by how I looked, not by how I performed. This brought to mind the question that had been posed to me many times, *"If I was walking the Spiritual Path, why even bother attending a university?"*

For me, education was about learning for the sake of learning. Though being spiritually innocent is a benefit, being uninformed seemed to serve little purpose. Though the established educational institutions are certainly not the only pathway to schooling—for me it seemed the appropriate road.

As I walked across campus mentally debating the occurrences of the day, I thought back to a time a year or two the previous. I was walking to the supermarket to buy some supplies for *the Integral Yoga Institute,* a spiritual community I was involved with. I was standing, waiting for the light to change on Sunset Boulevard in West Hollywood, when these two girls from the Midwest drove up. Seeing my long hair, long beard, prayer beads, and funny clothing, they asked, *"Are you a Hippy?"* I laughing answered, *"No, I'm a Yogi."*

When I returned to the center, I told my story to one of the sisters of the order. She said, *"See Shiva Dass, God was testing you."*

Choices

On *the Spiritual Path* you make a choice every day. You can choose to follow the ways of the world. Or, you can choose to follow the divine order of the universe and be spiritual.

This understanding certainly has nothing to do with how you are dressed, however. But, how you dress will delineate how you are perceived.

The Sikh wears a turban. This tells the world of their religious conviction. The Priest wears a collar. This lets everyone know of his or her avocation. But does what a person wears truly depict spirituality? No, it does not.

> *External is always external.*
> *External can never be internal.*

What you wear can tell the world something about the life you choose. It can even influence how you behave. If you are seen as holy, you may behave in a more spiritual fashion. Though all of this may be seen as an aid to spiritual progress, in actuality, it is not.

External image also leads to ego. The monk who wears robes is immediately treaded as a holy crusader, just as the military officer who wears a uniform is immediately seen to be a trained combatant and is treaded accordingly. To truly embrace spirituality, you must transcend the need to be defined by your external image.

The Job

This same premise leads to the perceptions many people have about working and spirituality. If an individual is enlightened and walking *The Spiritual Path*, then how can they have a job?

The other side of the issue is; if one doesn't have a job, how are they supposed to survive? Does enlightenment put a roof over a person's head and food in the stomach?

Sad but true—physical needs are the basis of life.

An ideal example of this is Ram Dass. When Ram Dass traveled to India on his quest for the truth about LSD and spirituality, he met a man named Bhagavan Das. Bhagavan Das led Ram Dass around India, introduced him to his to his *Guru,* Neem Karoli Baba, and basically turned Ram Dass on to the path he has followed for the rest of his life.

Ram Dass came from a very wealthy family. When he returned to the United States, he possessed the financial resources to live the life of a modern-day *Sadhu*—traveling and teaching. Bhagavan Das, on the other hand, did not come from this background. When he returned, he eventually began selling cars and then insurance. Was he any less spiritual because he had to work for a living? No. He just had a different road to follow.

It is essential to remember that spirituality is not defined by what you wear or what you do to survive. Spirituality is about who you are on the inside.

Bukowskian Zen

More than simply what you wear or what you do for a living is another level of refined consciousness that teaches the individual who walks upon *the Spiritual Path* to embrace all things as part of that path. This is to say, that even things which may be considered, by the unenlightened, as less than spiritual, are, in fact, quite spiritual, depending upon your frame of mind.

How many times have you listened to an individual criticize a person for being less than holy, stating, *"A spiritual person wouldn't do that."* The response I believe that should be voiced is, *"How do you know?"*

People who are not spiritual continually wish to judge and criticize another person's level of spirituality. Yet, a truly spiritual person never does this. Why? Because they understand the true essence of spirituality—that all paths lead to the same place—enlightenment. That everything you do is spiritual as long as you view it as a path of consciousness. I call this, *"Bukowskian Zen."*

For those of you who have read the works of Charles Bukowski, the words he writes details a life dominated by women, alcohol, and horse racing. If you read between the lines, however, there is something very spiritual about what he is portraying. He is living life at its root essence. What he is doing—he is doing one hundred percent. I know this because I was lucky enough to have spent some time with him in my Hollywood youth. Due to this fact, what he does becomes his meditation. And, who is to say that his method of meditation was or is any less valid than one who sits for hours with their legs crossed.

"Sitting," as it is known in Zen, may appear to be more spiritual. But, that is only because that is what has been programmed into the world mind as the measure of spirituality.

Spirituality and enlightenment are not something you can wear on your sleeve. Spirituality and enlightenment are something that comes from within. If you can get drunk and truly view it as a path to enlightenment, then who is to say you are wrong. There is a large group of *Sadhu* in India who use what is known as *Soma, "A drug,"* to aid in their path to enlightenment. In India they are considered holy, so who is to judge the path of the Western yogi?

This being said, there are an enormous amount of people who have not truly walked down *The Spiritual Path* who will questions this logic. But again, we come back to the main point—appearances are not what they seem.

Back to College

It took me awhile, but I left my orange robes behind. It took me a little while longer and I left behind the Sanskrit name and the *Yogi* clothing. Though I left behind these external images of my delineation, I never left behind the essence of being a *Sanyassin.*

My realizations about life and external images evolved. And, I moved forward. Though I discarded certain aspects of external spirituality—the essence of who I became so early in life has never left me and has continued to define my physical existence.

Though I eventually left behind the external images, this was not before I received a grade of, *"D,"* in the class from my all-knowing philosophy professor.

This man was the perfect example of the fact that perceptions are the basis for *Maya. Maya* is the pathway away from *Satori*. As long as you care about how you are perceived, you cannot perceive your True Buddha Nature.

Let go of perceptions and the world will be a much better place.

Let go of excuses; forget about how a person, situation, event, or even you appear.

Move past the external and embrace the essence of nothingness.

This is Zen.

Chapter 8

Enlightenment is Easy.
It's Life That's Hard.

You know you're famous when people you've never met say things about you that aren't true.

One morning, a year or so ago, I began receiving e-mails informing me that a Ph.D., based at a Midwestern university, had authored a document about me and had posted it on a martial arts on-line discussion group. One of the individuals who alerted me to this fact was nice enough to include a copy of the discourse in his transmission. As I read it, I could not stop laughing. The Ph.D. had gone to my website, taken brief passages, and then intermixed these statements, out of context, with his own negative appraisal of my life and my works. He really attempted to slam me.

Perhaps the most amusing thing, at least to me, was that he attempted to present his paper as a work based in scholastic fact—as he applied the necessary reference points to my website and other sources. Of course, he didn't mention the limited scope or the one-sided approach to his research. The reason this was particularly funny was that this paper was present about a person like myself, whose life is such an open book. In association with being amused, I was really amazed that a university employed Ph.D. would have even wasted his time writing such a limited dissertation. I mean, what was the point?

Though the individual who e-mailed this document to me was very upset—me, I loved it. *"The first expose' on Scott Shaw."* It was so *National Inquirer.*

As the day went on, I received additional copies of the document and other postings that this Midwestern Ph.D. had made about me over the past year or so from people who thought I deserved to know. In all cases, he really attempted to attack me.

I found it hilarious. I mean, the minute you accomplish something, there is always going to be those envious people who are going to try to bring you down. The people who had contacted me were not so amused, however. They attempted to post rebuttals on the website. The webmaster of the group apparently disavowed all of them and several of these individuals were blocked from possessing the ability to even access the group.

For several days I received e-mails about how angry these individuals were about the Ph.D. who wrote *the Scott Shaw expose'* and the webmaster who barred them from the group. One individual, who was an attorney, suggested I sue the author and the webmaster for libel. But me, I thought, *"How perfectly poetic."* You see, these events demonstrate the root source of why people do not interact with enlightenment—because most people choose to focus their *Life-Time* upon the lives of other people instead of refining their own consciousness.

Now, this goes both ways. Not only does it ideally depict the individual who bases his life upon negatively attacking others, as this person did to me, but it also defines the individual who chooses to worship a teacher or mythical being to the degree that they are left forever separated from higher consciousness due to being locked into the realm of worship.

The Meditation Class

I remember when I was about twenty-one years old, I was teaching the martial arts on a daily basis and one night a week I taught the meditative aspects of yoga in a course at the local University Extension. Several of the students in my class where also taking a course in *Kundalini Yoga* from another instructor. This *Kundalini* instructor expected the students to bring him flowers each class session as a sign of devotion. The students asked should they also bring me flowers. I laughed.

One particular couple in my class were about my age and were heartily walking *The Spiritual Path*. After class one evening they asked if they could have a private meeting with me. *"Sure."* So, a few days later they came by my apartment and asked if they could become my disciples. Again, I laughed.

You see; this is the problem with people in a position of power; whether it be a Ph.D. or a person who has walked *The Spiritual Path* for a long period of time—some of these people falsely believe they hold knowledge that others do not. And, they believe it is only they who can summarize this knowledge and pass it along.

But, this is ego. It is not knowledge.

If one lives in this state, and they pass their understanding along, it will simply be biased by their own sense of judgment and self-worth. It will not be the passing along of *True Knowledge.*

This is the entire reason I did not remain living in an *ashram* in India. Though you possess a great support group for your spiritual practices, those who visit the *ashram* or see you walking down the street in orange robes immediately identify you as holy. In India, they literally walk, or in some cases run up to you and touch your feet—hoping for a blessing. And, this is just because of the style of clothing you wear. But, holy is never external. Holy is only internal. Knowledge can never be given; it can only be experienced by the individual who possesses the mindset to understand the source of knowledge.

If this sounds complicated. It truly is not.

Teaching Without Teaching

At the root of Zen is the understanding that we are ALL already enlightened. It is simply the fact that most people do not realize this ultimate truth. Thus, they do not interact with *Nirvana*. Instead, people choose to spend their time wearing *"Holy"* and *"Knowledge"* as if it were clothing. But, this is never holy. In fact, if someone is wearing their degree or their ordination as an accomplishment, they are about as far from possessing *True-Knowledge* and *Divine-Understanding* as one can be.

This is where disillusionment in one's teacher is born. Either the teacher places himself upon an, *"All-Knowing"* pedestal or the student provides this pedestal for the teacher. Then, when the teacher is realized to be only human, (as we all are), they fall from grace in the eyes of their student and the student is left feeling foolish for once possessing a belief.

Modern Sages

The great modern sage, J. Krishnamurti, truly proved his ultimate understanding—he never claimed to be a teacher. By not claiming secret knowledge, he taught from a position of purity. Thus, this man's cosmic understanding cannot be denied.

Alan Watts, another great modern teacher, was a chain-smoker, alcoholic, and admitted womanizer. Yet, this did not stop him from possessing a truly deep understanding of cosmic reality and sharing it with the world. He did this without ever claiming enlightenment or stating that he possessed any more knowledge than anyone else. He was simply a vehicle.

Doing What You're Doing

You can go to India and become a *Swami*. You can go to a university and receive a degree. I did both. But ultimately, *"So what!"* That is just something to do. And, *"Something to do,"* is the condition of this place we call life. *"You must do something."*

This requirement of, *"Doing Something."* is one of the main sources of *Maya, "Illusion,"* as most people choose to do things from a very unconscious perspective.

We are all programmed, from youth forward, that we must achieve, that we must accomplish, or our lives will be meaningless—we will not have made a contribution. But, this is a subtle point on the path of consciousness—we are in a human body, so we must do, *"Things"* to survive. But, it is our state of mind while we are, *"Doing,"* that makes these actions either spiritual or actions simply lost to the meaningless ways of the world.

Ask yourself, *"Why are you doing what you are doing?"*

There is no right or wrong answer. It is only you who can come to a conclusion as to whether or not you are advancing universal spirituality or simply embellishing yourself and the entire world in more nonsense. This is an essential point that most people never take into consideration while doing what they are doing.

The World Begins with You

The world begins and ends with you. What you do effects so many unseen actions. Everything that you say, write, think, or do, sets a never-ending chain of events in motions. This is *Karma.*

Your actions can be positive, which will cause positive actions to emulate from you—which will make the world a more positive place. Or, they can be negative. What comes from negative is obvious.

Ultimately, you can either lay the building blocks of positivity and consciousness or set a row of dominos falling. It is your life. It is your choice. So, what are you going to do?

Chapter 9
What is a Cult Leader?

Ever since Jim Jones, his *People's Temple,* and the mass suicide that took place under his guidance at *Jonestown* in Guyana in 1978, Western Society, particularly American society, has become fixated upon the concept of a, *"Cult Leader."* Pretty much, since this occurrence, every spiritual teacher became the focus and they were all deemed, *Cult Leaders.* This is particularly the case if a spiritual teacher is of East Indian or Middle Eastern descent. Forget about it, they must be a, *Cult Leader.*

This trend was amplified with the birth of the Internet.

I was one of those people who was around this technological world before the internet was even called the internet, and I have witnessed this firsthand. This trend has particularly become the case with the onset of the numerous sites that present opinion presented as fact. Though they call themselves on-line encyclopedias and databases, they are far from it. In fact, there is so much misinformation and personal opinion, presented as fact on the Internet that it is almost mind-boggling.

In association with these on-line encyclopedia sites, there are also those sites set that are solely designed to present a list of well-known spiritual teachers. On these sites they put up all kinds of biased and one-sided information about these teachers, attempting to make them appear as *Cult Leaders.*

To be fair, in some cases, the people they describe are, in fact, *Cult Leaders*. But, in many cases, they are not. These sites are simply set up for shock value and to cater to those right-wing thinkers who want to find fault in all that is different.

Perhaps, the most interesting thing I find about this phenomenon is that the people who write and define individuals as *Cult Leaders* on these sites and on the pages of various journals have never even meet the people they describe. They base all of their writings upon secondhand knowledge.

What these writers do is to simply take a small section of words that a teacher has written or spoken, and then quote them, usually out of context, placing these statements in some overall dissertation about how the person is evil, controlling, and what an antichrist they are.

As someone who has experienced this style of personal review, more than once, I can categorically state that the conclusions this style of research reveals are completely false and misleading. Yet, as it is presented as fact, many people, seeking to live in a space of negativity and criticism, due to a personal lack of fulfillment in their own lives, will believe it to be truth. It is not!

From a more refined perspective, we can question, *"What are the people who are setting out on this path of character assassination and destruction actually attempting to accomplish?"* To answer, they are attempting to shift the consciousness and control the opinions and minds of those who read their work. Is this not what a *Cult Leader* does? So, in essence, they are walking down the same road as those supposed *Cult Leaders* they are attempting to Out.

Now, as stated, some people are *Cult Leaders*. They want to gather people around themselves so they can have sex, money, power, or whatever. But, from my own personal experiences, the majority of those people who have risen to the level of *Cult Leader* are of Caucasian descent and not East Indian or Middle Eastern. Yet, when a teacher is of Eastern decent and teaching a Spiritual Pathway, that is not Christian, they are immediately assumed to possess less than pure motivations. How ridiculous is that?

Perhaps the best questions to ask when initially attempting to define a *Cult Leader* are, *"How much does your church charge you to attend their services?"* I use the word, *"Church"* from a broad perspective. *"What is the price for you to learn what they have to teach?"* And, *"Are you willing to pay that price?"*

To Some Personal Experiences...

As is common knowledge, I spent a number of years under the guidance of Swami Satchidananda. In all of those years, I was never asked for one dime. In fact, just the opposite. Swami Satchidananda and the people who made up his organization fed me, took me places, were my friends, and were very nice to me. In all those years, the only time I gave any money to Swami Satchidananda was once. We had painted and cleaned up his room at the Los Angeles *Integral Yoga Institute*. The person in charge of the Institute asked the close disciples if they would like to donate some money to buy Swamiji a new quilt for his bed. So, I willingly donated a whopping ten-dollars. That was it. In all of those years, ten-dollars!

And, this was no different for anyone else who made up the group that formed the foundations of *the Integral Yoga Institute*. If people wanted to take yoga lessons, there was a very nominal fee of two-dollars charged per class. If people wanted to go and see Swamiji at one of his lectures, they paid the five-dollars, seven-dollars or ten-dollars to see him speak. That was it. All very fair.

Any money he may have congregated throughout his life was from the payments he received from his lectures. How is this any different than a person who has a nine-to-five job and has a savings account? His job was simple to teach people about the spiritual lifestyle. They could take what they wanted; agree or disagree, and that was that. There was never anyone trying to get someone to join the group or some secret sect attempting to suck people in. It was all on the surface. What you saw was what you got.

It was the same when I went to India and was living at *ashrams*. Nobody ever charged me anything. In fact, I came back from my first trip to India with virtually the same amount of money I had in my pocket when I arrived.

Spiritual people are good, they are giving, and they don't want your money. What they desire is to help people find meaning in their lives. And, this is what many people are truly seeking.

Finding meaning in one's life is the reason why people join spiritual groups in the first place. Whether it is the church, the army, or whatever. But, those people who want to define all spiritual teachers as *Cult Leaders* overlook this fact. They overlook this fact simply because these teachers are teaching something different than what is taught by the pastor down the street at the local Christian church.

I can tell you as someone who went to Catholic school for a period of time, the level of abuse: both verbal and physical and the level of brain-washing that takes place in those institutions is so intense. Yet, everybody seems to overlook this fact, excepts when it comes to a child being molested by a wayward priest or nun. Let's not forget the nuns. And, this has only come to the forefront of modern consciousness in recent years. I mean, Catholic school is a mess—talk about brain washing...

"Brain washing," that term always strikes a funny chord in me. Swami Satchidananda always used to joke when someone would ask him whether or not he brainwashed his disciples, He would question, *"Why? Does your brain need washing?"*

But, back to the point. I remember really negative people coming to *the Integral Yoga Institute* and saying, "I know all the people here are having sex behind closed doors." But no, they were not. The people who made up the environment were very honorable and very dedicated to a celibate lifestyle. Though some would eventually move on from the celibate lifestyle to that of a householder, none took their vows lightly. Whether Swami Satchidananda had sex with female disciples, I do not know. I never saw it. Though a very few claims came out years later. But, if he had sex, he had sex. It was a willing union. And, that is that.

The question can then be poised why does a group form around a specific individual at all? Well, just as when you go to school you study under someone who has mastered the subject. It is no different with a spiritual teacher. People who are drawn to *The Spiritual Path* congregate under a teacher who teaches the lessons they wish to learn.

So, is a spiritual teacher automatically a *Cult Leader?* No, they are simple a spiritual teacher. When you have completed the class and learned what you needed to learn, you leave. I did.

Chapter 10
The Conflict of "I"
and the Spiritual Path

I remember the first time that I sought out *the Integral Yoga Institute*. This was the center for the teaching of Sri Swami Satchidananda. I was very young and I showed up at their door in the early afternoon. A very nice female *Swami* greeted me. She invited me in.

She returned to her position of sitting on the floor, folding and stapling flyers to be sent out regarding an upcoming yoga retreat. I asked, *"Do you need some help?"* She said, *"Sure."* So, we sat there talking, folding, and stapling.

It wasn't long before another female *Swami* entered the room. The two soon left the room, as I continued folding and stapling the flyers. From the other room I could hear their conversation going from discussion to yelling. They begin to scream at each other. I sat there, continuing to fold the flyers.

Now, this verbal confrontation went on for quite a while. As a young adolescent, walking *The Spiritual Path*, I could not help but question the relationship between these two Swamis and to ponder the question, *"Was their behavior spiritual?"* And, *"Was this a place of spirituality?"*

Eventually, I finished all the flyers. I sat there contemplating leaving as the argument continued. But, soon the first Swami reemerged, all smiles.

As the years went on, and my relationship with *The Integral Yoga Institute* grew, I became very close to this Swami. She was a truly nice and very spiritual person. Occasionally, we would joke about that early event and how she and the other Swami just could not get along.

We Are Who We Are

I began to realize early on my Spiritual Path that there is conflict. We are who we are. We like what we like, dislike what we dislike. This is not to say that what we like and what we dislike is not based in desire. Because it is. These two female Swamis could have been, *"Big Enough,"* to leave their difference behind. But, at that point in their evolution, they were not. This does not make them bad or unholy—simply controlled by what they like and what they don't like.

"Likes" and *"Don't Likes"* are the human condition. This is why the Buddha said, *"The cause of suffering is desire."* Because we are all based in desire. And, desire is a subtle and virtually invincible enemy to spirituality—especially when we walked down the roads of the world.

Rank

The ironic fact that I realized through my years of close involvement with the *Integral Yoga Institute* and the Martial Arts is that, with rank comes power. With power comes ego. And, ego leads one away from *the Spiritual Path*. The ego of others is what eventually caused me to leave *the Integral Yoga Institute*.

Now, *hand-in-hand* with the Westerners who became *Swamis* in *The Saraswati Order* of Sri Swami Satchidananda, was an ongoing debate of power and control. The term, *"Swami Power Trip,"* was often unleashed.

This was due to the fact that for the most part, most of those who entered the order came from an emotional position of, *"Lacking."* Once at the IYI they were immediately handed purpose and position. With this, not only were the roots of spirituality given birth to, but also so was spiritual ego—which is perhaps the worst kind of ego, because it is so cleverly hiding under the guise of, *"But, I'm Spiritual!"*

Advancement

Advancement is part of this human condition we call life. At every level, accomplished is dangled in front of our noses. *"If you are not this, you are unworthy." "If you have not accomplished that, and been given a title, then you are just not up there with the big-boys."* Or, *"I am this, I hold this title, this means you are lower than me."*

This is one of the primary problems I have with monkhood and the various levels of definition associated with *the Spiritual Path*. I mean, people aspire to be Gurus, Priests, Swamis, and Nuns. They do this so that they will be, *"Something." Something other than Nothing.*

I remember how later in our friendship, the female Swami detailed that before she found Swami Satchidananda and become one of his monks; she used to be a *"Complete liar."* She jokingly stated, *"I used to lie about everything."*

Now, I think we all have known people like this—people who simply lie to lie. To each person they tell a different story.

What is this psychological condition based upon? It is based in the desire to be something, to be more. So, when this lady became a Swami, she,

"Became." Thus, she was, *"Something,"* and no longer had the need to lie.

The problem with this whole mindset is that it sets a world of competition in motion and continues the process of conflict. Which is why great souls like J. Krishnamurti left behind many of the trappings of spirituality. Yes, he was a spiritual teacher. That was his job. But, he did not define himself with robes and titles.

The Downside of Achievement

One of the big problems with this world of achievement is that the moment a person achieves something, there will be others who try to tear them down.

Modern society, particularly those who inhabit the non-spiritual world, love to witness the demise of people of stature. So, here is perhaps one of the most important points of *The Spiritual Path*, *"If you do not desire position, if you do not claim position, if you are not teaching a doctrine, then who can come at you and attack you for doing anything?"*

Ultimately, why can a person be brought down or criticized? Because they claim titles, position, or knowledge. If they did not, then what could be taken away?

Now, this is one of the subtle elements of life. Life is about doing. You cannot—*Not Do.* Energy permeates this universe and our bodies. It is the energy of constant movement. So, *Not Doing* is not an option. But, how you, *"Do,"* is the essence to *a Spiritual Life.*

Doing

In my world of *Doing,* I have commonly followed a path of artistic creativity. This has taken many forms, but perhaps most notably is that of writing and filmmaking. Now, writing is pretty much a solitary craft but though my filmmaking, I have met many people—*some nice, most not.*

Though filmmaking I have also come to have many revelatory experiences—particularly those that involve the individual and the concept of, *"I."* In fact, in many of my films, I either have the character I am playing or another character make the statement, *"So, what's in it for me?"*

This statement is a joking reference to the world of acting and filmmaking in general. That world is so ego based and most of the people involved in it are so self-absorbed, that all they can do is think about it themselves.

You

In Hindu yoga ideology there is the philosophic concept that, *"You,"* are the center of the universe. In fact, it is believed that there is no external people, places, or universe at all. It is simply a project of your *Thinking Mind.* The *Thinking Mind* is, of course, the root of, *"I."*

Whether or not you accept this concept is not really important. But, what it does demonstrate is how people, even those who walk *The Spiritual Path*, are so, *"I,"* based that they cannot get out of their own way long enough to witness the true perfection of this place we call, *"Life."*

Most people are so, *"I,"* orientated that they believe that everything that is going on in the world has something to do with them. I mean, I get e-mails and letters all the time from people who have read something I have written and believe that it was directed, directly at them. When I read what they have to say all I can do is smile, because not only do

I not know who they are, but also what I wrote had nothing to do with them.

Now, this is a *Life-Problem* in general in that most people are so lost in their own *I Consciousness* that they project all kinds of thoughts and opinions onto other people. They start *Thinking* and then draw conclusions about what another person must be thinking and feeling about them and their specific actions. The reality is, what a person thinks or does not think is simply a *Mind-Thing*. It is not a defining factor for life. In fact, the only reason anyone cares at all about what another person is thinking is because they want to be perceived in a specific fashion by the individual, they are projecting these thoughts upon. This is the ultimate reflection of *I Consciousness*. But, *I Consciousness* is not *Self-Awareness* or *Self-Realization*.

Giving

This, *"I,"* ideology also goes to the source point of giving. People continually turn to other people for gifts, guidance, and help. It is so common that a person goes to someone that they think is better, richer, or more holy and asks them for, *"Things,"* be they material or ethereal. Even in my life, people are continually coming into it and asking me for something: to put them in movies, to add them to the crew of one of my films, to put them in photos in books or magazines, to write a blurb for the back cover of their book, or to just help them out and give them *Life-Purpose*. But, the reality is, no one ever comes and offers me a helping hand or asks me what I want or need.

Here, again, this fact gives reference to the root problem with the outside perception of accomplishment. The way people perceive my life is through their own eyes. Whether or not their perception is accurate goes to individual circumstances. But, the reality is, I have not accomplished anything that others have not done better or that anyone else cannot do if they try. Yet, by having accomplished what I have accomplished no one ever offers me anything, but they ask me for a lot.

This is the problem with the, *"I,"* mentality. People see externals. They witness the *Outside.* But, they do not seek the *Inside.* And, this is the problem with those driven by the, *I Consciousness.*

I Consciousness is a curse and leads to all kinds of problems and conflicts. This is because of the fact that what people's, *"I,"* believes, and what it causes them to do, has a direct effect on the lives of others. Oftentimes, this effect is very negative.

Murder

When I was thirteen or fourteen years old, my mother and I visited her hometown in the Midwest. By this point in time, I was already a vegetarian and was very focused upon walking *The Spiritual Path.* One of my much older cousins was an avid murderer. (Did I say that?) I mean, an avid hunter.

One evening, he and my mother would not take, *"No,"* for an answer, when they decided that they wanted me to go, *"Coon Hunting,"* with him. Though I was very upset, my elders had made up their mind. I had no choice.

We arrived at the backwoods of Illinois. He unloaded his, *"Coon Dogs,"* loaded his rifle, put on his hardhat with a light attached, and walked off.

Though I had known this man for virtually all of my life, I had never seen him like this. He instantly became crazed. He would see the eyes of a raccoon studying at him, and bam, he would shoot it out of the tree. It was then the job of his dogs to go and retrieve the dead animal.

Now, this killing was not for food or clothing, or anything like that. It was solely for fun. In fact, he would just take the dead carcasses his dogs had retrieved and throw them into wood. How barbaric is that?

He was darting through the woods. Me, with no flashlight was struggling to keep up.

He had guided us to a small creek. He jumped over. I attempted to follow, but with no flashlight, I misjudged this distance and found myself knee deep in thick mud. I grabbed onto the branch of a near by tree and pulled myself out. In the process, however, I lost one of my tennis shoes. One of my new gold-suede *Converse All-Stars*. I remember them well. And, though I tried to retrieve it. The mud was far too dense.

Normally, I would have found this very amusing. My cousin was so *hunting-crazed,* however, that there was no way he was going to stop his quest for murder. All I could do was to follow, to the best of my ability, running through the woods with one shoe and one sock while gunshots went off. My one foot, without a shoe, was obviously getting very trashed, due to the heavy forest growth.

The one good thing that came out of this experience was that one of his dogs, stayed very close to me—as if he was my guardian angel.

My cousin would be somewhere off in the distance. I would sometimes see his hardhat light and hear his shots. I would try to follow, hoping that a bullet would not come flying in my direction. In essence, I was completely lost. Yet, all that night, the dog stayed next to me.

Hours past and finally it was over. I was told to return to my cousin's International Harvester jeep. When I finally found my way back, instead of being appreciative that his dog had stayed with me, protecting me and guiding me, my cousin beat the dog for not finding any dead raccoons that he had shot. How messed up was that?

I obviously grew a very strong bond with this dog. I tried to convince my mother to let me purchase the dog from my cousin. But, she felt that an apartment in Hollywood, California was no place for a, *"Coon Dog."*

Sadly, I never saw that dog again. But, I do often remember how the pure soul of that dog was willing to take a beating to protect me.

You see, this is the sad element of human life. People do what they desire—guided by developed *I Consciousness.* They do what they do, and they become so engulfed by their own desire for fulfillment that they do not care what devastation they may have unleash upon the lives of others, (animals included), and the world around them.

The biggest problem with this type of *I Consciousness* is that this style of behavior is accepted by the masses, and, in fact, stimulated.

This previous story relates primarily to animals, but this type of crazed behavior happens all the time with people, as well.

A number of years ago, I was driving by a 7 11 in Redondo Beach, California. In the parking lot was a man being harassed by another man behind the wheel of his car. The one man had apparently, inadvertently, walked in front of the driver as he was attempting to pull out of his parking spot. Verbal insults were exchanged and the man was threatening to run the other guy down with his car.

Obviously, there was a lot of male machismo fueling this situation, but the guy remained standing in front of the car. The man behind the wheel was now lunging his car at him.

A couple of spectators started yelling, *"Hit 'em! Hit 'em!"* Finally, spurred on by the gathering crowd, the driver did. He plowed into the man with his car. The guy was smashed onto the ground. Just then the police arrived. Soon after, so did the ambulance. But, this whole scenario goes to show how people set a course of life-action in motion, driven by an *I Consciousness* that has no basis in *Goodness;* only driven by ego and power-tripping.

From this, they negatively alter the lives of other people, and, in fact, have a very strong possibility of negatively altering their own life by falling prey to this type of non-refined action.

This is just wrong. Each person has the ability to choose what they do, how they live, whom they associate with, and what they are going to do with each set of circumstances that they are presented with it life. From this, they either walk through life leaving a trail of conscious good or they perform negative actions and leave a long list of negative *karma* behind them.

The Bird & The Dog

Maybe six months ago, I was about to enter a shop on Pacific Coast Highway and I looked to the intersection and there was a small bird that had apparently broken its wing and was fluttering around in the street. Though I didn't know if I could save it or not, I impatiently waited for the light to change so I could run in the street and at least get the bird out of the street. But, the moment the light changed, this aging Latin man in his beat-up pickup truck intentionally ran over the bird. I stood there torn with sadness over the needless loss of life, as he drove off laughing to his friend. I mean, how much life has been killed in this world based in this same needless Power Mentality?

Then yesterday, I was driving South on the 101 Freeway between Hollywood and Downtown Los Angeles when this little brown dog darted out of nowhere and began running next to my car down the freeway. He ran out onto the freeway. I stopped. I jumped out of my car attempting to save him. My actions luckily caused him to run back onto the shoulder of the freeway. This while other drivers were honking and yelling, *"Fuck you,"* at me.

I mean, where does someone have to be that is more important that the saving of a life?

In reality, there was a part of me, the inner-city street kid who grew up on the wrong side of the tracks, who was very willing to stare down these people and tell them, *"Fuck you,"* right back. But, this is where spiritual discretion comes into play. And, this is the most necessary element to understanding the spiritual life, while stepping away from the control hands of, *"I."*

Just as the great East Indian Sage, Sri Shankaracharya detailed in his work, *Vivekachudamani, "The Crest Jewel of Discrimination,"* refined spiritual discretion is one of the most key elements to elevating one away from the *I Consciousness.* Thus, guiding them towards enlightenment.

Criticism & Compliments

Those people who were honking and yelling, *"Fuck you"* at me is the same point of manipulation where people try to control others through criticism.

They hold the belief that if they speak negatively about a person, discredit their thoughts or their ideas, then maybe they will come around to their way of thinking. But, who are they to extend judgment over anybody else's life? And, just as occurred with my two Swami friends, commonly all criticism equals is conflict.

In essence, criticism and compliments are the same tool of manipulation. The reason people pay compliments to another person is also to gain a source point of control over them in order to manipulate their actions. But, it is only a person who is so locked into the deceptive elements of the, *"I,"* ego that they let themselves fall prey to these levels of emotional deception.

People Don't Care

Now, this is one of the primary problems with life, *"People don't care."* That is to say, they don't care about anything but themselves. All they care about is their own momentary reality and how they feel or how cool and in control they look in that particular moment.

And, the sad reality is, you cannot make people care. You cannot make people think. You cannot make people accept a spiritual sense of reality. Because, people don't care about anything but themselves, their things, and what they want.

More Pronounced Domination

When I was twenty-one years old, I had a very serious motorcycle accident. It was Sunday afternoon and I was traveling to Hollywood to visit my mother for dinner. As I drove along Burbank Blvd., from my apartment in Encino, a female driver turned left into me. I went flying off of my motorcycle, ultimately highly damaging my left knee, right ankle, right foot, my shoulder, my face, and fracturing my skull in several places.

I am told, for several days the doctors thought I was going to die. But, with the help of some very skilled surgeons, obviously I did not. Thankfully, I do not remember most of it. But, the lifelong damage to my body was done.

I remember my first day out of the hospitable. I sat on my mother's couch realizing that my life was never going to be the same. My body was trashed and I was in a lot of pain.

Me, all I wanted to do was to get back to teaching the martial arts and yoga to my students, finish my university degree, (that was only one semester away), and to live the life I had once known. But, at the hands of another, everything changed.

I believe what is most revealing about this situation, at least to how it relates to this essay, is that the woman who hit me was more concerned about herself, and how what she had unconsciously done to another person, was going to affect her own life.

She obviously didn't care about what she had done to me. She never even attempted to say, *"I'm Sorry."* Instead, she was so locked into *I Consciousness* that when the lawyers got busy, she attempted to sue me. Obviously, she did not come out on top. But, it just goes to show how there is so little compassion in this world for anybody but one's self and their own momentary reality.

This situation details how people only think about their own *Life-Situation* and not what they have done or are doing to others. And, that is a very sad fact about this modern world.

Make it a Positive

Though I had long been aware of the understanding that we must see and embrace the fact that, *"It is all perfect."* It was at this point in my life that I forced to see this philosophy in a more expansive manner.

One of the small, *Life-Things,* that occurred, due to this situation, had to do with music…

As many youths are, I had been very involved in the music of my generation, and I was an active musician. This especially came into focus with the birth of Punk Rock in the mid to late 1970s.

The first generation of punk rockers had kept the long hair that had become the norm of rebellion in the 1960s. Due to do my necessary brain surgery, however, they had shaved my very long blood-soaked hair. So, there I was with no hair.

By this point in time, however, the trend in Punk Rock had begun to change. Now, anyone with long hair, (except for members of the Ramones), were ostracized. Thus, I allowed this bad situation to open the door for me to experience a new world that I would not have been let into had my hair remained long.

Now, this is a very small point, to a very big issue. But, it is important to note that when bad things happen, when people do bad things to you, you cannot let them win. You must take these small victories and help them to redefine your life. Thereby, keeping you mind focused on the positive and not the negative that has been unleashed upon you.

Bishop, California

As I seem to be telling some stories about my life here, I guess I can tell one more...

112

Maybe fifteen or twenty years ago, the person I considered my closest friend in the world, invited me to watch the bicycle race of his stepson in Mammoth, California. The first leg of the race began in Bishop, California.

Now, I didn't really want to go, but he and his wife insisted. So, I gave in. I packed up my girlfriend. We jumped into her car. And, away we went. But, by the time we were outside of Bishop, which is a small town in shadows of the Eastern Sierras, something was very wrong with her transmission. Though the car was less than a year old, it died on Highway 395. We had it towed into town. But, as we soon found out, Bishop was a small town. There was no one who could work on her transmission.

I told my friend of the condition. Now, here is the funny point about *I Consciousness*. Instead of saying, *"Well, I have to go to this race but let's leave your car here, get a tow bar, and pick it up on the way back to L.A.,"* or anything like that, his response was, *"Sorry man, this is my only vacation of the year. There's nothing I can do."* This, after twenty years of friendship! He left me stranded!

So, there we were, my girlfriend and I, stuck in Bishop, California. We had to stay in a small roadside motel for a few days, waiting for a tow truck driver willing to take us back to L.A. And, I had to pay the tow truck driver the last six hundred dollars I had to my name to get the car back to where it could be repaired.

Though I was in disbelief about my long-time friend's actions and choices, it was not that I did not understand. He had a new wife and a new family, and his priorities had changed. But, his choice of noninvolvement was not the, *"I,"* choice that I would have made.

But, that is the story of life and *I Consciousness*. Unless a person is willing to put aside their own opinions and desires, *I Consciousness* becomes the controlling hands of everything. With, *"I,"* as the defining element, then power and control become the delineating factor of life. At this level the world is set into a pattern of unresolved conflict and everybody's life that it touches becomes worse not better.

This is why the individual who walks *The Spiritual Path* embraces *Karma Yoga. Karma Yoga* witnesses you doing all that you can do for the betterment of life, society, and the world. And, making the world a better place never involves control, death, or destruction—that's politics and power, not conscious action.

Karma Yoga is also never based in a personal concept of giving a person or persons what you think they want or need in a specific moment in time. Because that type of thought process is only based upon the controlling hands of personal-opinion. And, personal-opinion is never formed from an enlightenment mind.

Instead, *Karma Yoga* is based in the understanding of *"Surrender to Betterment." Karma Yoga* involves stepping beyond, *I Consciousness*. This means that you may have to give up what you personally think or want in any specific moment of time—because ultimately you come to understand that what you think or want in this moment will not be what you think or want in the next.

By surrendering what you want and by giving instead of taking you donate to the overall *Betterment of LIFE*.

We Do What We Do

We have all done good things, and we have all done bad things. We all have said things that we did not mean. We all have said things that came out wrong. We all have done things that we regret. We have all NOT done things that we wish we would have.

This is a condition of human life. This is also the place where the person embracing the path of consciousness separates themselves from those who exist totally in the space of *I Consciousness.*

We have all made our share of what we believe to be mistakes. But, this is where the person who walks the path of consciousness separates themselves from those who simply justify their actions and pay homage to the ways of the world.

The conscious person makes a mistake, realizes it, and grows from it—never to make it again. In fact, in most cases, they attempt to remedy what or whom they wronged. The un-conscious person, on the other hand, doesn't care what effect they are having upon others and, thereby, continues to live in a world dominated by *Self*—making mistake after mistake and commonly not even realizing or accept responsibility for the mistakes they have made.

A Trail of Positivity

Each of us sets a course of actions and events in motion in our lives. These actions and events come to define our legacy. Some people leave a trail of positivity, while others leave a wake of negativity.

For those people who have created much negativity, they can change their actions at any stage of their life. But, most do not. They simply embrace their path and never falter from it. This is why I believe that you can usually know a person fairly quickly upon meeting them. Simply look at the trail of the life they have lived.

Giving

Ultimately, the path of consciousness is defined by giving. The adverse is defined by not giving.

An ideal example of this occurred in a situation with my aforementioned friend and his brother, a year or so ago. His brother left his longtime job. He was a new father and was desperately in need of employment. When he approached his brother, the brother refused to help him. I asked him why he would not give his own brother a job. His response was, *"Why should I hire him? I can hire Mexicans who already know what they are doing for $8.00 an hour."* A pretty harsh statement…

Now, one must look at the back-story to truly understand this situation. My friend has had two primary jobs in his life. I arranged the first one, when we were still teenagers. In this job, he was taken in and given extensive training that no new employee had ever received. This occurred due to the fact that my mother was one of the key executives of the company and she was the one who ushered him into the business. The second job he had, occurred under similar circumstance. He was taken under the wing of a family friend and, again, was given extensive training, and immediately put into a position of authority—though he had no background in the industry. Yet, when his own brother came to him and asked for help, he rejected him. I could not help but wonder what *karma* that created?

People Do What They Do

People do what they do. What they do does not make the necessarily bad or good. It simply makes them a representative of a specific element of consciousness.

The person locked in *I Consciousness* cannot or will not, step beyond their own momentary concept of reality. Though each of us has an untold number of factors that has created who we ultimately have become, the person of consciousness always attempts to help others and to make this world a better place by helping those in need. The person locked into the realms of *I Consciousness,* on the other hand, does their *Life-Things* solely for, *"I."*

Where Do You Live?

Where do you live your life? Are you giving or are you taking? Are you arguing or are you accepting? Are you destroying or are you creating? Are you helping or are you hurting? Are you daydreaming about what things and accomplishments you want to make in your life or are you surrendering your desires and giving back to the world? Are you making your space better or are you making the world better?

Who are you?

Chapter 11

Open Eye Meditation

When people hear the word meditation, the first thought that pops into their minds is the image of a person sitting crossed legged upon the floor. Though this image of mental silence and tranquility has come to define meditation, in many ways this definition limits the true understanding of this process. Meditation is much more than simply sitting crossed legged, focusing your attention upon a mantra or watching your breath.

I believe that it is an essential element, on the path to realization, to bring meditation into your everyday life. If you simply, *"Sit,"* and turn off for a specified amount of time every day, you may bring calm into your everyday life, but you will not make everyday life your meditation. For this reason, I believe we all must learn to meditate with our eyes open.

To achieve this, you must train your body and mind to make the actions you do a Meditation and not something that you are simply doing. Now, this gets a little complicated, and it is a bit different for every individual who enters into the path of *Open Eye Meditation.*

To begin, you must first define your own level of reality—what is it that makes you, you. What do you do with your *Life-Time?* How do you do it? And, how do your actions affect not only you but also the world around you?

This is a very essential point. You must define how your actions effect the world around

118

your—because if your actions: be it your hobbies, your job, or how you treat other people exist in the realms of negative, then no matter how much you formally meditate, you will experience little positive growth. The reason for this is obvious—negativity breeds negativity. Therefore, the first step you must take, before you can bring *Open Eye Meditation* into your life, is that you must release any action that cultivates negativity and replace those actions with the opposite—positivity.

The Process

For each person the process to *Open Eye Meditation* is different and can ultimately only be defined by you. For who knows you better than you do?

This being said, once these preliminary elements are out of the way, you must move forward and start to make your *Life-Time* a meditation.

The Job

As detailed, for each individual this is a different process. And, this process will change at different points in your life. For me, an interesting experience occurred when I decided the best thing I could do to test my skills of *Open Eye Meditation* was to get a job.

To say this will make many people exclaim, *"What!"* Because they have spent their entire life dominated by one job or another. For me, my path through life has been different. Certainly, I have taught yoga and the martial arts forever. I have taught at several Universities and Colleges. I was a model in Japan, Hong Kong, and occasionally in the U.S. I have been a radio DJ in Bangkok, a musician, an artist, a photographer, a writer, an actor, and a filmmaker. But, I never had a *job-job*. I have never worked *nine-to-five*.

Many of my friends, throughout the years, would comment as to this fact, *"You don't know what it's like!"* So, when I was presented with an opportunity to exploring this level of existence, I decided I must go and find out—experience what has dominated so many people's lives.

Motivation

To understand my motivation for this, I remember when I was in my late twenties and my mother, who was a very traditional person, kept saying to me, *"You really need to get a job."* Now, this was not based on my need for money. It was simply based in her traditional understanding of the world and the way she thought that life was supposed to be lived. My response was always, *"My Time is all that I have! And, I refuse to give My Time to someone who will make money from my actions and not give a damn about me!"*

Perhaps this was a naive statement. But, it was how I felt. So, as you can see, a job was probably the best way to test my *Open Eye Meditation* skills.

The Audition

My motivation for this adventure was presented to me when a friend of my applied for a job at a particular company and was turned down for employment. My friend laughingly told me, *"You are exactly the kind of person they are looking for."* So, almost as a joke, I create a resume and mailed it off. A few days later I was called. The person on the other end of the phone was very friendly and asked about my writing. At the end of the conversation, she invited me in for an audition and asked that I bring some samples of my writings.

The funny thing is, (at least to me), is that I had never been to a job interviewer before that moment in my life. I used to jokingly refer to them as auditions—because I had been to a lot of those in the world of acting. So, I put on a suit, (pretty much how I dress all the time anyway), grabbed a few of my books and a few magazines I had written articles for. I was off...

L.A. being L.A., the commute to the job took me about forty minutes at off-traffic time. So, I could not help but think what I was in for if I got the job—a lot of time driving on the freeways.

I arrived at the company, and everyone was very nice. It was so smiley-smiley I could not help but wonder, *"Was this some kind of cult?"* I auditioned for several people—each asking several questions about my education, my writing, and a few asking why a highly published author, like myself, would even want to have a job. My answer was, (and it is true), *"We all have to survive and unless you are Steven King or Jackie Collins, you don't get rich from writing books."*

The entire process took about four hours. I was placed with a few working people who actually did what they were going to ask me to do. Overall, it went very well. I was finally dismissed.

As I drove home, I received a call. *It happened that fast...* They wanted to hire me ASAP. Now, I truly do not know why. I was very surprised. Was it my Ph.D., my *Books-in-Print,* or ??? I could not help but question their decision, as I had no experience in the world of JOBS. In fact, they offered me more money than I had asked for.

As a means of subliminal protection, a way to keep myself out of a job, I had asked for quite a large amount of money for an entry-level employee. I'm not going to disclose the amount. But, it was not *chump-change.* The fact is, they were going to pay me an amount that many workers only dream about. That, plus full-on benefits, etc.

A funny note: I have this tradition that when I am auditioning for a part in a film that I do not want, I intentionally act very badly. I do this, so the casting director will have a reason <u>not</u> to cast me. An ideal example of this occurred when I was called in for a martial art film several years ago. Now, there was no way in hell I wanted to be in this film, though it was high-budget and it starred a fairly well-known martial art actor. As I always joking tell people, *"The only bad films I'm in are my own."* But, my agent was insistent that I go, as the production company wanted me to be, *"The Bad Guy."* So, I went. I thought I had thrown the audition away on the first interview, but I got *a callback.* This time, I had to do the scene in front of the producer and the director. So, I had to really throw it away! Which I did. I acted the scene out very theatrically—loudly and badly, like you see in the movies of the late 1930s.

Going to this job audition was like that. I tried to say all the wrong things. But, somehow it did not work. I was booked for the gig...

The Fear

As is often the case with *Open Eye Meditation,* there will be a lot of trepidation prior to the beginning of the process. This is especially the case when you are entering into a new realm of existence in order to test your own level of consciousness.

122

Every bone in my being told me to not show up on the following Monday morning. *"This is not who I am! I am not a worker!"* Like this one filmmaking friend and I used to jokingly scream out when encountering the small-mindedness of the world, *"I'm an artist god damn it!"*

But, without putting yourself to the test, how can you define your cosmic understanding?

The alarm rang early Monday morning. I suited up. And, off I went... As detailed, this is pretty much how I dress anyway.

The first test was that they have a rule you can't wear tennis shoes. As that is my normal style and has been forever, the first delineation of my *Open Eye Meditation* came into play, I had to wear hard shoes.

The Training

The first step of the job was to learn their highly defined process of using their in-house computer system that was based on a very old system of DOS. Me, being a MAC guy from way back, I hadn't used DOS in maybe fifteen years. But, as I play with Windows on the side and remembered the old days of having to enter codes to get a response, I possessed the foundations.

As I was being told about the codes, this is where my mind really began to rebel. I just didn't want to learn them! It's like the process of formal seated meditation—for many people it really takes a long time to train the tiger of the mind to be able to turn off your thoughts long enough to actually encounter the sublime reality of cosmic interaction. Many, when they are in seated meditation, simply learn how to pretend. They train their body to be seated quietly, but their mind is still traveling a thousand miles an hour—racing from thought to thought. That was me at that moment. I just didn't want to do it! I walked outside at lunch and pondered, *"What a concept, being told when you were supposed to eat and when you could take a break. How very monastic of this place..."* Mostly, as I walked outside, my *Thinking Mind* became very upset. I was screaming to myself, *"This is a complete Brain Fuck! What a waste of life!"* I even wrote a poem to that effect.

Back from lunch came the next slap. Though I had hoped to remain anonymous at this job, by the first day, the fact that I was an author, actor, and filmmaker had spread though out my workplace. One, (really nice), guy comes up and says, *"Since you're the resident celebrity can I ask you a question..."* Now, this really pushed my buttons because I knew everyone was discussing me. And, I hadn't said anything to anybody. In fact, I had avoided all questions about my life except to the interviewers. And, to them, I was as brief and as nondescript as possible.

I was sure they were all pondering why a guy like me needed a job. Well, I didn't! Similar to the statement my friend and I used to scream in jest, I wanted to blurt out, *"I'm doing this for enlightenment god damn it!"*

All of this was amplified by the fact that my other, *"Real Life,"* was calling. I had an article due. I had to read over the final proofs for my new book. And, I had to complete the final edit on my most recent film, as the distributor wanted it NOW!

Me, I was *Stressed-Maximus.* One would think that I could have picked a better time to put my *Open Eye Meditation* to the test. But, if it were easy, then it would not be a test.

Foundations

This is the foundation of *Open Eye Meditation*: If it is going to be easy, if it is going to be enjoyable, then it is not a meditation at all.

That is not to say that *Open Eye Meditation* must always be difficult, because that is not the case. Once you get comfortable with this process everything becomes a meditation. It is simple that sometimes you must throw yourself into the fire, like I did in this case. Sometimes you need to test yourself.

Training Continues

The training continued. Several, (all very nice), people taught me. This one man, perhaps fifty years old, came to speak with me. What provided me with new insight into my *Open Eye Meditation* was the fact that he totally defined himself by his job. His wife or his children did not define him, nor did any outside interests—*he was his job.*

He gave me a detailed history of each occupation he had. This reminded me so much of my mother. My mother was completely defined by her job. No matter what was going on in her life or the life of her only child, she would wake up at 5:30 AM every day and prepare for her job.

This may have been the causation factor for me guiding my life away from the, *"Working-world."* I mean she was oblivious to all the hell I lived through in my youth—because it was all about her job. My father was not very different—as a *restaurateur,* business owner, and later a high-level arena manager, he had little time for anything but his job.

The man, who was describing his life to me, proudly exclaimed how he had even moved his family across the country from L.A. to the Midwest and then back to L.A. all for his job at this company that I was now working for. Yet, all he could detail, regarding his children, was how they were not as driven and motivated as he was.

Having had a similar experience in my own life, (which I will detail in a moment), I wanted to say, *"I wonder why? Don't you think that maybe your moving and the multiple doses of culture shock they experienced had something to do with it?"* But, I was sure anything I said would have fallen to deaf ears.

The Lessons

You see, this is the path of *Open Eye Meditation*—you must be willing to take in all that you experience and allow it to bring you to a clearer perception of *Self*—while still remaining conscious. These lessons are learned by not only taking conscious notice of your own reaction to life experience but also by listening to the experiences of other people.

This is the hardest part for someone who has not walked upon *The Spiritual Path* to comprehend and the main reason that the individual on *The Spiritual Path* walks a different road than others. On *the Spiritual Path* you are constantly reminded that you must stay conscious—you must be interactive with the cosmic energies of this universe. But, for those who have not walked upon *the Spiritual Path*, life is all about, *"Needs,"* defined solely by the, *"Desires,"* possessed in the moment.

A Student

An ideal example of this existed with one of my adult martial art students maybe twenty years ago. This man was fifteen or twenty years my senior. He was a very nice guy and one of my first black belts. He worked at a body shop and did his job very well. But, the shop closed and he freaked out because he was completely defined by his job. What occurred was that he packed up his wife and belongs and headed back to his home state of Georgia. He did this before the dust could even settle. He never even tried to look for a new job. He immediately assumed that he would never be able to find another job and he would complete fail. He just wanted to go back to a place of safety and lick his wounds.

Now, I have seen this same type of behavior in many people, including my mother, when my father died in 1968. I was ten years old.

My father passed away just before Christmas 1968. My mother, who came from a very dysfunctional family, (long before this term was ever coined), was originally from Illinois. When my father died, she immediately sent for her older sister—who arrived the next morning. My mother and I were in an obviously tearful mood. My aunt walks out of the bathroom that morning and brazenly states, that my father had come to her in a vision and stated, *"Stop all this bullshit crying!"* Well, there went any period of mourning I had—only one day… After that I was not allowed to cry over the death of my father. My mother then sent for my uncle and on Christmas day 1968 I was driven to a relative's house near the Mississippi River where they cut my hair and told me I could no longer wear love beads. Remember, this was 1968. I lived with them throughout the Winter and Spring months—an eternity to a ten-year-old. My mother arrived in June after selling our home in Southcentral Los Angeles and dealing with all of the business she felt needed dealing with.

Now, the situation was slightly different for my mother than it was for my black belt student. The job she loved so much was still waiting. So, after a couple of weeks or maybe a month, my mother realized her addiction was just too strong. So, we climbed on an airplane and headed back to L.A.

We arrived at LAX in the early evening. The sun had just set. As was the case in the 1960's sometimes rockets were launched from a nearby Air Force based. The sky was etched with orange and yellow swirls—created, I assume, from remaining rocket fuel.

As if God had a paintbrush, it looked spectacular. It was very artistic.

Looking at Consciousness

The sad thing is, most people live their entire life based in the space of lack of consciousness. They are solely driven by emotion and desire.

It is essential to understand that both emotion and desire keep us separated from understand the more subtle realms of this place we call life. In fact, most people have a never-ending plethora of excuses for their desires—few ever realized that their life is driven by desire. They simply assume they have made this or that decision and that is the end of the story. But, there is a big problem with living life from this position of existence. From this mindset comes one of the primary reasons people are kept from the path they were truly meant to follow. For the individual who should be walking *The Spiritual Path* or the path of art, life circumstance and the desires, of not only one's self but those envisioned by others, create the foundations for life. Due to this fact, most are unable to break free and embrace their own true essence. For those who choose the ways of the world, well that is their choice and their life may turn out good or it may turn out bad. But, as they are not making a conscious positive contribution to this *Life Place,* they are simply passing between birth and death and little more can be said.

Witnessing the Process

When I first started this job and was detailing the, *"Smiley-Smiley-ness,"* of the company to a long-working friend of mine, she said, *"You just wait and see, that it not how it really is—at every job there's politics."* I kept this in the back of mind and walked on...

Within the first week at the company, I came to realize that their system functioned, but it did not really work. This is to say, there was no one answer. If I asked the same question of four different people, I would get four different answers. This truly surprised me with a company of this size. At our first department meeting, about two weeks into my stint, I mentioned this fact. It was amazing to see the level of denial that went on from the management. But me, the new kid, I was the living proof. At the meeting I also noticed that no one else spoke up when asked for comments. I later realized that I had committed the ultimate *faux pas,* criticizing the structure of the system. I also realized the reason no one spoke up is that they were so fearful of losing their job that no one dare to say anything. As I passed the waiting area of the facility, I understood that this point was driven home on a daily basis by the fact that the company was constantly interviewing potential new employees.

By the third week I begin to clearly witness the politics that were in play. My friend had warned me and she was right. It was very subtle, but there was a lot of fear about saying the wrong thing, doing the wrong thing. It was kind of like watching the cartoon, *Chip and Dale, "Excuse me. No, excuse me."*

At lunch one day one of my coworkers told me how people were fired. A supervisor would go and get the person and walk them to the door while another supervisor packed their things. They were then escorted out and the door was closed. I mean, how fucked up is that! And, I was now certain that people were fired for all kinds of nondescript reasons.

By my fourth week, I felt my *Open Eye Meditation* had run its course. From a personal perspective, I had learned a lot. The first thing was that I realized that within the walls of a job life passed by so quickly. I mean hours would go by and I would not even realize they had passed. A day would be gone. And, it was gone forever—*never to be lived again*—with nothing accomplished. I understood how people grow old at a job having never lived. They wake up one day and they are old and their life is gone. The other thing I realized is how fast money goes. One of my *Open Eye Meditation* missions was to live solely on my wages. I would get paid and it would be gone before I knew it. So, I also realized how people would come to the end of their working career and be dependent upon the small amount of money that *Social Security* pays.

"I Quit!"

The, *"I quit,"* point came on Thursday morning one month into my *Open Eye Meditation*. Now, I had been waiting for the appropriate moment because I was sure I would be walked to the door before too long—more to make a statement about firing, *"The resident celebrity,"* than anything else.

The day before, during my lunch break, my agent called and told me that I had a wardrobe fitting as I had been cast to guest star on this television series. The only problem was they wanted me there in two hours. Normally, this would not have been a problem. But, with a job...

My agent said, and it was true, *"This gig is going to pay you more in one day than you would make in one month at that place."* (As money is what Hollywood people base their lives around). She was right. But, I have always tried to be a considerate and conscientious individual. So, it was hard for me to make the decision. But, I did. I went in and told a supervisor I had to leave. She gave me a very dirty look. But, I was gone.

I had heard stories about the, *"Take no days off,"* policy of this company. So, I knew if I were to take off for the T.V. shoot they would have a reason to fire me. I debated on Wednesday night whether or not to go back at all. But, I did.

Early in my session on Thursday morning, the guy who had come up to me and commented, *"Since you're the resident celebrity can I ask you a question,"* came up and invited me into a private room. He was a supervisor. He was very nice. We made small talk, then he asked about my rapid departure on the previous day—prefacing it with the, *"Politically Correct,"* statement, *"You don't have to tell me if you don't want to."* The conversation went on for a while and it was all-good unit he said, *"One more thing..."*

The Back-Story

To tell the back-story—one of the company's managers, one of the people who had actually interviewed me, was gone—gone without a trace. There for years and gone. That tells you a little bit about the loyalty of this company. *"My supervisor,"* went around the department the morning she was gone and told each person individually that the person would no longer be there. When she came to tell me, my joking nature came out and I said, *"I'm just waiting till you walk me to the door."*

What a back-stabber, *"My supervisor,"* had relayed my joking comment to the *powers-that-be* making it sound like I was trying to slam the dismissed employee. Perhaps the most interesting thing about this situation, at least to me, was that I had listened to *"My supervisor,"* make rude comments behind the back of several other employees. I guess she knew I wasn't the type to say anything and posed no threat. I obviously discovered that I could not say the same thing about her.

So, I was about to be, *"Talked to."* This was especially enlightening, as the joke I made was all about me, not about the person who was out the door. I truly felt for that person. *Me, my life is an ongoing joke—a mystical comedy.* But, for that person, they were instantly out of a job—fired. I'm sure that did not feel good after dedicating their life to a company for so many years. And, how was that person going to explain their being expelled to the next potential employer when they applied for a new job?

Back-Stabbing

I believe that backstabbing is one of the worse things you can do to a person. The problem with backstabbing is that it has the potential to truly disrupt a person's destiny. Thus, it creates negative *karma*. It is as Dante Alighieri detailed in his work, *The Inferno,* betrayal of trust is one of the ultimate sins.

I remember several years ago when a friend of mind, who I had brought into the world of filmmaking, backstabbed me with two distinct people—one right after the other. Now, I knew he had done this because after he had talked to them—instantly, my relationship with these people degenerated to zero. The problem was I truly felt that I had a destiny to live with each of these individuals. I simply had certain *Life-Stuff* to consciously clean up before I could move forward. But, through his words, my opportunity to move forward with these people was taken away.

Life is a Dream

Have you ever had the experience when you are dozing off to sleep, and you begin to enter into a very specific dream? Then, all of a sudden, a noise or something wakes you up. As you drift back into sleep you enter into a totally different dream. You see, this is the process of life. You enter into the flow of destiny from where you are. If someone or something interrupts this flow, then your course is altered forever—it can never be lived again. And, this is the problem with backstabbing—it interrupts people's destiny.

It is almost irrelevant what motivation a person holds for backstabbing. Because, undoubtedly, each person who backstabs is going to have a justification for what they have done. But, this does not change the fact that backstabbing is based in insecurity and misplaced ego. It is a means to exert nondescript power over another person. It is a malicious act. From this can only be born negative *karma*.

In the case of, *"My Supervisor,"* I am sure her actions were a method to reaffirm her commitment to the company, so she could hold onto her position of employment for a little while longer. As I really didn't care about the job, I found her actions amusing and a reminder about how we must always remain acutely conscious while practicing *Open Eye Meditation*—as you can never anticipate what you will encounter. My friend, on the other hand, wanted to reveal what he believed to be some deep dark secret about me to these people. Though he may have thought he was doing them a favor, if he would have looked deeper, he would have realized that he was simply unleashing a negative act—attempting to remove opportunity from my life for whatever self-motivated reason.

Now, this is the sad part about his actions and backstabbing in general—because who possesses the ultimate wisdom to know who should know what about any person's life at any particular moment in history? From his actions he took away situations which may have equaled something truly positive, not only for me, but for himself, and the rest of the world, as well.

I remained his friend even though I knew what he had done—because that is what friendship is: accepting the bad with the good. I would jokingly say to him every now and then, when the subject of these two people came up, *"I know you told them..."* He would always deny it until he got into therapy and began to become more in touch with himself. But, by then, it was too late. The opportunities and the chances were long gone.

One day, while we were having lunch at a beachside cafe, many years after the fact, he said to me, *"You know, my life really ended when we stopped making movies together."* I was very surprised to hear that he felt this way. But, this was the perfect example of how backstabbing *karma* came back to haunt and define a person's life. Though he did what he did, said what he said, for whatever personal reasons, and I held no ill will towards him, he set a course of events in motion that ultimately ended our filmmaking partnership— which obviously had a very negative effect on him.

You see, this too is an element of *Open Eye Meditation.* In life, we must interact with people. People are people and they are going to do what they are going to do—motivated by any number of reasons and ideologies. We must stay conscious of this, accept that life is life, and then grow as a person by learning what not to do when various life situations are presented to us.

Here again, we go back to the root point of consciousness; when people live their life at a negative level attempting to pay homage to ego or the *powers-that-be* while disrespecting others, every person around them is removed from a space of conscious purity and forced to live in a world of competition. Now, some may say that survival of the fittest is the root of climbing the corporate or worldly ladder. This may be the case in corporate America, but it is not the case of spiritual consciousness. To live at a spiritual level, you must do all you can to help all of humanity and remove the nonsensical realms of *Maya,* which permeate the world. Feeding them only creates negative *karma* and negative *karma* leads only to negative ends.

Honor

But, back to the storyline...

As I sat there listing to the guy detail the policies of the company, I realized that the environment was permeated with negative *karma*. I understood that the people there, including this individual, had no honor.

A person without honor is never worth associating with. For a life without honor is meaningless.

I mean, he sat there talking about the fact that the individual who had gotten fired was his friend—that they were carpool buddies. Yet, he stood by and did nothing when his friend got fired. Nothing, except to defend the policies of this company.

A person who supports a nondescript entity, like a job, over a friend has no honor. He cared more about keeping his job than his friend. And, that is just not right! Because, at the end of the day, all we have is our friends and our family.

"My Supervisor" also had no honor. She too cared more about keeping her job than a person. So much so that she backstabbed me over nothing—making what I said appear to be more than simply a joke about me.

The Company had no honor because they trained all of the employees to lie to the customers and tell them that *out-of-stock* parts would be in their hands within two weeks. This was the case even if the part was gone to *never-never-land* forever. This was obviously done so the company could keep money flowing in.

The sad thing is few people even care about honor—few even understand what honor is and why it is so important.

As the person spoke, it was as if a mystical veil of illusion had been removed from me. I realized that this company had no honor and it was run by people who had no honor. I could remain there no longer.

That was it! I stood up. I smilingly told the guy, *"I quit."* A look of complete disbelief came over his face. I shook his hand. I walked out the door. I was gone...

Smiley-Smiley was, in fact, not so *Smiley-Smiley.*

You never know, had the *Smiley-Smiley* been real, I may have stayed there forever—become a worker bee. But, I guess that is just not my destiny.

Understanding Open Eye Meditation

When it comes to *Open Eye Meditation,* it is not always going to be as contrived as the situation I created for myself regarding a job. Many times, for any number of karmic and social reasons, we are going to be driven into a place that we truly would rather not be in; i.e. me as a child being sent to Illinois for six months. The reality of this is—this is life and things are going to happen that we do not want to happen. For this reason, it is essential that you train yourself in the techniques of *Open Eye Meditation.* From this, when these situations occur, instead of making them wholly negative, you can tune into your *Higher Self,* transcend the world of the common process of basing all of your life upon the way you DESIRE things to be, and transcend to the realm when you can interact with cosmic conscious and perhaps come to understand why you are living what you are living.

To Each Their Own

As the old saying go, *"To each their own."* There is no one method or single technique for *Open Eye Meditation.* The Buddhists will tell you to *Sit* and watch your breath. The Hindus will tell you to cross your legs and recite a manta. These are the techniques of formalized meditation that have been laid down for centuries. The Buddhists even have walking meditation—but this is not *Open Eye Meditation.*

In *Open Eye Meditation* you must remain conscious, focused, and transcend the limitations of your desire. How you ultimately achieve this can only be defined by you—because *Open Eye Meditation* is not as simple as simply *Sitting* for meditation. It is different in every case—different for every person. To this end, you must do what you do while creating a conscious connection to the divine. Each time your thinking brain takes over, like mine did exclaiming this job is a, *"Brain Fuck,"* you must refocus your consciousness, bring it back to your center, and continue walking down the path of *Open Eye Meditation.*

Why?

The question may be raised, *"Why perform Open Eye Meditation at all?"* Why? Because it tests you. It allows you to define the subtle areas of comfort you have defined for you own life. With this knowledge, you can push the boundaries of *Self.* Push the *Self* to *Universal Self.* With this, you can bring enlightenment into every aspect of this place we call LIFE.

If *more-and-more* people do this then, *Everyday Enlightenment* will spread across this physical world, and all of humanity, if not personally embracing it, will at least be interacting with those of *the Enlightened Mind.*

Chapter 12

I Was Born in L.A.

I was born in Los Angeles, California in the late 1950s. I grew up during the turbulent 1960's in a portion of the city that has come to be commonly referred to as Southcentral L.A.

In 1965, this area exploded with the Watt's Riots. The memory of the National Guard, in their tanks and troupe carriers, patrolling the street, and watching the news reports of the carnage that was taking place is etched into my mind. It was a time of chaos when the redefinition of American society was unfolding.

Perhaps this isn't such a unique experience, as there were obviously an untold number of people living in that area of L.A. at that historic period of time. But, perhaps what is a bit more unique is the fact that I'm Caucasian with blonde hair. Whereas the average person occupying that vicinity, at that period, was Africa-American.

I remember my first day of first grade. I walked into the classroom, looked around, and realized that I was the only person not of color. Now, this was a shock for me because I had gone to Kindergarten at a Christian school and there were a variety of ethnic categories that had made up my peer group. But, as I had transfer to public school, I immediately found myself standing out from my surroundings.

It was not that I did not establish friendships. But, being called a, *"Honky"* or *"White Paddy,"* being attacked by older children, and being challenged to fights, by several children at a time, due to my skin's color, was almost a daily occurrence.

When I tell people about my early childhood, the question is immediately asked, *"Was I from a very poor family?"* In fact, I was not. It was simply that my father had grown up in South-central L.A. and for him it was the world he had always known. He had not taken notice that the area had changed.

My family and I lived in South-central, with the commonness of the previously described experiences, until the day Martin Luther King Jr. was assassinated. A gang from the nearby junior high school decided that due to the fact that I was the only known white person in the vicinity, the murder of this great man had to be my fault.

So, the word was out—I was going to be killed.

My schoolmates continually walked up to me that day, with smiles on their faces, telling me that the gang was on its way to get me. I was going to die, like Martin Luther King Jr. had died.

I was eight years old...

That entire day, I was constantly reminded that the gang would get me as I was walking home. The fear I experienced permeated my entire being and it was devastating.

That afternoon, I began my walk home. And yes, as I looked down the street that I traveled each day, there they were. They were rapidly approaching—in quest of me—the only Caucasian that they knew of.

I ran back into the school. The police soon showed up. They must have been made privy to the rumblings of the community, as well. They were there to take me home.

And yes, as they drove me home in the back seat of their police car, we passed about twenty members of the gang yelling and screaming at me.

Upon arriving at home that day, the police officers were astounded to find that there was no one waiting for me. They found it hard to believe that each day I waited at home, by myself, until my mother arrived from work. *None-the-less*, using our phone, they called my mother and told her that it probably wasn't a good idea to send me back to school until things cooled down. Probably not...

Soon after that my father died. My mother and I moved to East Hollywood. From the frying pan into the fire as it were.

Though I moved frequently during my late youth and early teens, I eventually ended up in *Virgil Junior High School* on Vermont Ave., where the majority of the populace had changed from Black to Latino. Gangs were everywhere. And now, we were adolescents and things had gotten much more violent in the few years that had preceded my Martin Luther King Jr. experience. Again, outnumbered and hated by the masses, I was accosted on virtually a daily basis. It got so bad that I had to ditch gym class everyday due to the fact that every time I went into the locker room I was sure to get jumped by several gang members—as they never came at you *one-on-one*. Of course, I never told my aging Caucasian gym teacher of my experiences. So, he just gave me an, *"F,"* on my report card.

Failing gym class. And, they said it couldn't be done...

I'm certainly not looking for any sympathy by talking about the predicament of my early life. In fact, these experiences came to define the individual I have become. I just believe that I have a unique view into the mind of prejudice—something that the non-Caucasian races have undoubtedly experienced, to varying degrees, throughout the history of this country. But, how many white people have encountered this style of ongoing fear and confrontation, simply due to the color of their skin? Not a lot I would imagine.

Prejudice is a funny thing. It is born in a mindset of anger and rage—for what has happened, what could happen, and what may never happen. It is an emotion founded in the most animalist level of human existence—for it has no basis in fact. It is only derived from ignorance.

When I first read this essay to a friend of mine she said, *"Nobody will want to hear this. It is too politically incorrect."* Her being of Asian descent and growing up in America she did, however, immediately identified with my situation.

Politically incorrect, maybe it is. But, if we can't look at our society from a realistic point of view, how can we ever overcome the lack of humanity that so many people face each day of their lives. The young African-American or Latino male, who is stopped on the street by the police, simply because they fit the profile of a gang member. The women who is hounded by the construction workers hanging off of their job site and yelling at her as she walks by. The elderly individual who is hounded by young hooligans as she struggles home from the supermarket, attempting to carry her meager groceries. And, on yes, the young white kid who grows up in the ghetto who is hated for no other reason than the color of his skin.

Chapter 13
Who is Spiritual?

The question has eternally been pondered, *"Who or what is truly spiritual?"* Certainly, if we look to history, we see that religion has been one of the leading causes of war throughout time. *"The conquest of the infidels,"* has been the motivating factor for armies to unleash their wrath by an untold number of despicable means. And, this process has continued into the modern era.

At the root of all conflict is an animalistic instinct for power, which mankind has yet to overcome. Sadly, this seeking of power has often been utilized by those who use God as their motivating force.

Certainly, the belief in God or a higher power, (by whatever name), is what has given humanity a positive central focus. This essence has provided mankind with the potential to transcend to the Higher Mind. Unfortunately, two things have occurred in association with this quest:

1. Some individuals who have walked upon *the Spiritual Path* begin to be adorned by other spiritual seekers.

2. An individual falsely uses God and spiritually as a means to an end.

As such, the association with God that many spiritual teachers possess allows them to do whatever they want to people and their actions are believed to be justified. Therefore, who is truly spiritual?

If we step beyond these obvious injustices, the root of true spiritually becomes even more difficult to define. In many cases, it can only be assessed by the individual and their particular level of cosmic evolution. Perhaps this is where all the problems begin, because spiritually is ultimately only assessed by the person. And people, by their very design, possess the inherent ability to be influenced by any number of factors.

This being said, let's get down to business. What is and what is not spiritual?

Looking to the Past

The late 1960's and early 1970's was a great time for spirituality in the West. The reason for this is that it was so accepted. The men and women all had long hair. Men wore drawstring pants. The women wore long skirts. Nobody shaved. Everybody wore *Malas, "Prayer Beads."* And, due to the fact that this image was so common, people were truly allowed to explore their spirituality.

The foundations for this had been laid by the Beat Generation of the late 1940's and early 1950's. By the time the mid 1960's rolled around—the world was ready. By the 1970's, it was in full swing. For those who possessed the spiritual inkling, opportunities were everywhere. This exploration led many people to Eastern Mysticism—by a number of names.

Tame Yoga

Personally, I remember when I was a young child; I was so drawn to the teachings of yoga. I first witnessed the postures being performed on Public

Television by a man named Richard Hittleman. While other children, of my age group, were mesmerized by cartoons and reruns of, *The Dick Van Dyke* and *The Andy Griffith Show,* each day it was, *"A Must,"* that I watch and practice the asanas and meditation in front of the T.V. And, I am sure I was not the only one.

Hittleman's teachings of yoga were tame by many standards. Yet, they were exactly what opened the door for many Westerns to delve into the deeper realms of spirituality.

Was Richard Hittleman spiritual? Yes, of course he was. He provided a great service by introducing the Western World to the understandings of yoga.

Interestingly, the Western World has witnessed a rebirth of this style of, for lack of a better word, *"Tame Yoga."* Schools of yoga have sprung up all over.

I remember just a few years ago, schools of yoga were few and far between. They had completely fallen from favor over the previous two decades. Now, like Starbucks, they are everywhere. Certainly, we can trace the yoga indoctrination of America to individuals like Richard Hittleman.

Moving Forward

Throughout the 1960's and 1970's people were allowed to embrace their spiritual roots. For some, that meant joining one group, staying with said group until such time as one encountered disillusionment, or just became disinterested, and fell away. For others, they had the dedication to stay on throughout their life.

This is where the true essence of spirituality is tested. In how long you remain.

Certainly, I am not saying that if a spiritual teacher wrongs you or you find fault in the teachings of a particular group that you must stay around. What I am saying is that if you are truly on *the Spiritual Path*, you must hold fast to it—this may mean changing teachers, but you never lose your focus.

The Sufi Order

Elemental to the early years of my spiritual growth was Pir Vilayat Inayat Khan and *The Sufi Order*. Though I had heard of them for a number of years, it wasn't until I was sixteen years old and had a car that I possessed the means to explore their teachings.

I remember going to *"The Dances of Universal Peace,"* which were then known as, *"The Sufi Dances,"* for the first time and just being blown away by the joy and meditative spirituality they instantly brought into my life. Everybody I encountered was so nice. In fact, the guy who picked up the two-dollars participation fee at the door gave me the ceremonial flower from the evening. The first flowers I was ever actually given. I took them home, put them in a vase, and received great spiritual revitalization from them each morning as I headed off to *Hollywood High School*—as I anxiously awaited the next week's dances to commence.

The thing about *The Sufi Order* that initially both surprised and intrigued me was that it was a much more loosely supervised group than the other spiritual groups I had encountered. Some people smoked, many held hands, people flirted, hugged a lot, and so on. I mean this was great. People were allowed to be who they were—as opposed to being forced into a sterile structure of celibacy, intense vegetarianism, and judgment about whether or not they were truly behaving correctly.

There is a downside to the less than structure spiritual lifestyle, however. Perhaps the most definitive moment of this came to be illustrated to me a few years later.

Sex and the Spiritual Path

As time progressed, I became a *Sufi initiate* and the doorman, collecting the two-dollars for people to participate in *The Sufi Dances*. Yearly, I also helped *The Sufi Order* operate a booth at *The Renaissance Pleasure Faire*. *The Renaissance Pleasure Faire* takes place in both Southern and Northern California. As the name implies, there is a lot of drinking and debauchery going on. This is especially the case once the faire closes to the public in the evening and only the participants are allowed to remain.

The lady who led *The Sufi Dances* had helped out this one particular weekend. She had spent the night. Her boyfriend had gone home to his Long Beach, California apartment. Upon arriving the next morning, he discovered that she had slept with another man. *"Bam!"* The boyfriend popped the guy in the face and threw a generalized fit. Can you blame him? The lady, on the other hand, became mad at him for being mad at her.

You see, this is where the problem of undefined spirituality comes into play. Certainly, anyone can do anything they want. This is your life and you can do whatever you want with it. But, if you walk upon *The Spiritual Path* you need to ask yourself what effect your actions are going to have upon other people.

The unconscious person does whatever they want—motivated by whatever desire is present. The individual on the path to consciousness needs to possess a more clearly defined and refined mindset than this, however. This is what sets the individual on *The Spiritual Path* apart from those who walk the path of the world.

Initially, this event stunned me. In fact, I stopped going to *The Dance of Universal Peace* because of it and refocused my *Spiritual Path* upon the more ascetic realms of spirituality.

I believed, *"If the teacher can't be greater than the student, what do they have to teach?"*

As time progressed, however, I thought back to words that Swami Satchidananda spoke to me years before. He stated, *"I have noticed that those people who are initially the most austere are the one's who always seem to fall away from the path."*

So, was the lady who led *The Sufi Dances* spiritual? Of course, she was. How could all of the joy she has brought to people by teaching them *the Sufi Dances,* thought out the years, be diminished by a choice she made which only truly effected three people: her boyfriend, her lover, and herself.

This is why we must all develop the ability to step outside of ourselves and learn not to judge. Because what truly makes a person spiritual? Is it what they do to themselves or what they give to the world?

Judgment

Judgment always seems to be a tool the, *"Less than holy,"* pull from their bag of tricks and unleash.

I remember how this local Los Angeles television show, hosted by George Putnam, (a right-wing newscaster), had invited Swami Satchidananda to be a guest.

As I was close disciple at the time; myself and a small group of my fellow disciples accompanied our *Guru* to the station. Once on the air, it was obvious they had set a trap for *Gurudev*. There was another guest who was set up to disrupt anything Swamiji said. Putnam kept going to this guest to refute all of Swamji's words. At one-point, Putnam states, *"Oh, I see the Swami's getting upset."* Baited, Swamiji answered, *"No, feel my pulse."*

This is the problem with judgment. We all have our opinions—developed from whatever source. Then, we create life situations that will actualize our previously conceived notions. Most, not as obvious as the previously detailed scenario, however.

The un-spiritual person is so willing to attack and judge the understandings of another simply to justify their own, previously obtained, beliefs. The spiritual person, on the other hand, is the one who must be willing to accept.

"Acceptance" is the key word to *the Spiritual Path*.

Many Teachers

Taking this understanding a bit farther, it must be understood that here are many teachers on *The Spiritual Path*. Many of them have been forced to hide their true personage or actions due to the fact that they are protecting themselves from unnecessary judgment.

Certainly, we can look to Ram Dass who was forced to hide his homosexuality from the world for a number of years to keep from being judged. Science now teaches us, however, that an individual sexual orientation is much more biological than choice.

The question must be asked, *"Is hiding your true nature spiritual?"* No, it is not. But, as in all cases, if you judge the actions and/or choices of another—judgment is only judgment. It is not true spiritualism. So, if you are judging, you are trapped in the space of the un-spiritual.

A paradox, perhaps. But, an essential understanding of *The Spiritual Path*.

Hiding

Many of the modern *Gurus* have been accused of sexuality impropriety with their disciples, including such great sages as Paramahansa Yogananda and Swami Satchidananda. I remember a story being told to me by an East India disciple of Swami Satchidananda, many-many years ago. He was from the same region of Tamil Nadu, India as Swamiji and he told of how our *Guru* used to go off with this one particular woman. I related this story to other disciples. They, of course, became enraged and dismissed it. But, this man was the witness, and he was still a disciple.

Whether or not this story, or the other accusations were true, I will never know. But, did this story bother me? No, it did not.

I think the only problem with sexuality and true spirituality exists when people on *the Spiritual Path* attempt to hide or lie about their sexuality. They attempt to hide behind a, *"Seemingly Holy,"* cloak of celibacy. From this, they are forced to make excuses once they embrace this natural desire.

Of course, aberrant sexual behavior is never justified—no matter how seemingly spiritual an individual may be. I am referring to consensual adult interaction. But, was Swami Satchidananda and is Ram Dass spiritual? Of course, they are. Both of them helped to usher spirituality into the minds of the masses.

It is only judgment that keeps anyone from seeing this.

The Cloak of Spirituality

This brings us to an essential point; the way spirituality is, *"Suppose,"* to be expressed and represented is perhaps the most debilitating element on the spirituality path. From this, people are cast into living a life of pretense—a life where they must pretend to be something in order that they will be perceived in a particular manner, so that they can teach what they have to teach. And this is about as far from spirituality as you can get.

Yet, there is the other side of this—when an individual truly is who they are... If we look to the life of Alan Watts, for example. Now, here was a man who was an admitted womanizer, loved to smoke, and was an excessive alcoholic. Yet, he hid none of it and he was still a great teacher of spirituality.

He was who he was and that is as spiritual as you can get. Because he smoked and drank will never diminish his contribution to the world of modern spirituality.

This reminds me of a funny story, if I may look back to my years with Swami Satchidananda again. Several members of the Los Angeles *ashram* were upset at this one disciple, due to the fact that each morning he would wake up and instead of meditating he would make coffee. He believed that because Swamiji drank coffee that it was all right if he made it in the *ashram*. A small group of us were sitting with *Gurudev* this one particular morning and the subject was brought up. *Gurudev* immediately began laughing and stated, *"That's why I don't live at the ashram, because I like coffee."* In other words, if you are going live in the *ashram* you must behave in a certain manner. And, this is an important point for life. You choose where you live and how you live. If you are going to live in an *ashram,* you must behave by the standards of the *ashram.* If you are going to live in the world, you must define what spirituality is to you and how it is best expressed.

My belief is that you must let go of the pretense of how spirituality is supposed to be expressed. Then, each person is allowed to be who they are—whether they are celibate or not—drink coffee or not. From this, each person is then allowed to express spirituality to the world in their own unique manner.

Osho

Perhaps one of the truest, (at least to himself), *Gurus* to have emerged in the last century was Osho, Bhagavan Shree Rajneesh. He propagated his love for sexuality and hid nothing. Whether or not you agreed with his path is almost irrelevant. He did what he did and never attempted to hide it.

When I meet Osho in Poona, India, in the late 1970's, he instantly overturned my brainwashing that the only true path to enlightenment was via celibacy. Was I set free? Yes, I was.

Was Osho spiritual? Yes. Were his teachings spiritual? Of course. Did his method of teaching have a price? Yes, it did. But, that's what happens when someone possesses a voice that is heard and they speak of revolution.

It's All in the Name

A funny occurrence happened to me concerning defined spirituality.

I received an e-mail from a man who worked at *The Bodhi Tree Bookstore* in West Hollywood, California. *The Bodhi Tree* is perhaps the Mecca of spiritual bookstores, as it was one of the first and remains one of the best bookstores geared towards the spiritually minded. In the e-mail the man asked me for one of my photos to hang on the wall of *the Bodhi Tree*. I was both flattered and a bit surprised at this request. But, as *The Bodhi Tree* sells most of my books, I happily went out and purchased a picture frame, placed one of my photos in it, and sent it off. A few weeks later I was in the store. I walked around and noticed that my photo was not hanging on the wall. When I went up to the cash register to purchase a book, I jokingly inquired as to where was my photo. The lady went back and asked the owner. She came back with the response, *"The guy who requested your photo made a mistake, we only hang photos of holy men on our walls."* I laughed.

I took note of the photos that surrounded me. Something I had done periodically over my thirty years of frequenting the store. The majority of them were of East Indian *Yogis* and *Sufis,* with only a few Westerners. For the most part, the photos of the Westerners that hung upon their walls were all know by Sanskrit names. I smiled as I walked out of the *Bodhi Tree* that day. I laughingly thought to myself, *"I guess I should have continued to use one of my spiritual names: Shiva Dass, Akbar, or Swami Mokshanada. Then, perhaps they would have considered me holy enough to actually put my photo on the wall..."*

Understanding Spiritual Judgment

People judge spirituality by what they hear about a person, by which preconceived notions they already hold, by what a person wears, by what name they are called, or by what they want to believe—good or bad. But, is judgment spirituality? No, it is not.

There are those individuals who will understand that your experience is your experience. They may not have a similar experience or agree with you—yet they accept. This is true spirituality. Then, there are others who will get in your face and argue that you are wrong, unholy, and a complete idiot if they don't agree with you. Here lies one of the subtlest, yet most deeply rooted problem for those claiming to be on *the Spiritual Path*.

An example of this occurred for me a few years ago when I used to answer all of my e-mail—even the ridiculous ones. This one individual contacted me, and we had a nice exchange of ideas. In one of my responses to this person, I attempted to explain an event that had occurred that day in my life. I received a response just blasting me. I don't even remember all of the negativity that was unleashed. But, it was deep.

If you allow yourself to be open, however, each life event, even the seemingly negative ones, can be a great teacher. For example, this interaction made me re-realize something very essential for this modern age—which is of particular importance when you gage a spiritual teacher. What I experience is not what you experience. My realizations can never be your realizations. And, yours can never be mine. This is especially the case when attempting to communicate something so subtle as a spiritual understanding with words. Sometimes, meanings and intentions are lost in the words. When meanings are lost, judgment is set into motion. When judgment is active, enlightenment is out the window.

Spirituality is everywhere—just as everyone and everything is spiritual. Let go of your judgment and you will understand this. Let go of your judgment and you will be free and you will allow everyone else to be free, as well. Then, questions like, *"Who is spiritual,"* will never need to be answered.

Chapter 14
"I Know More Than You!"

This place we call, *"Life,"* is a curious phenomenon. In association with all of the unwanted events we have to deal with; be they natural catastrophes, lying politician, or just the generalized reality of the unwelcome things that happen that we don't want to happen—we must also deal with other people. And, this is where life gets really interesting.

How have many times have we each encountered someone who defines themselves as better or more than us simply because they believe the life they are living is somehow more accomplished, more worthy, or simply superior?

"I am better than you because I don't eat meat, I don't drink coffee, I don't drink alcohol, and I do yoga!"
Or, *"You are a sissy because you don't eat meat, don't drink, don't take drugs!"*

These individual rationales continue:

"I know more than you and because I went to a better university than you!"
"I live in a better neighbor than you do."
"My race is better than yours!"

On *the Spiritual Path* this style of nonsense occurs, as well.

"I can meditate longer than you."

"My religion is the only true religion of God!"
"My teacher is more holy than your teacher!"
"You practice Cowboy Zen. I am a practitioner of Real Zen!"
"Jesus is the only true way!"

And, the martial arts, *Oh, my God,* it is saturated with, *I'm Better Than You Judgment?*

"Your style sucks! My style is superior!"
"Your techniques are terrible. My techniques are so much better!"
"I can kick your butt! Let's fight!"

Who of us has not encountered this style of *I'm Better Than You Judgment?*

Now, it is not simply that these people are out there and we happen to meet them. In many cases, we invite these, *I'm Better Than You* people into our lives. For example, people who practice psychology are some of the worst proponents of judgment ideology. What's worse is that they are provided with the license to do just that.

The problem is that even though people who study psychology may be doing what they are doing from a perceived perception of service, they are basing their assessments upon their own set of reality—not upon what is, *"The Truth."* They judge a person by what they've been taught or have come to believe is, *"The Truth;"* delineated by what they perceive they have come to know about a specific individual. But, the reality is, no one can ever truly know another person. They are simply being provided with a distilled set of experiences.

The fact is, even in psychological settings, people only reveal what they want to be known about themselves. Even if the patient is telling a psychologist the truth about themselves, as they believe it, this truth is dominated by personal ideologies, emotions, and gained understandings. Thus, it is not *"The Truth,"* as any relayed experiences are dominated by the individual's perceptions and understanding about a specific set of circumstances and about the other people who inhabited that set of *Life-Circumstance.* This is why psychology is a very flawed science.

Many psychologists are schooled to believe that they have some key to other people that the rest of us do not possess. But, a psychologist only possesses a very limited amount of information about the true psyche of any specific individual. They only know what they are told. And this, in most cases, leads to more problems than it solves. *None-the-less*, by being awarded a degree, a psychologist is provided with a basis for, *"Accomplishment Superiority."*

"What happened in your childhood to make you feel like that?"
"You're experiences are based in insecurity"
"Maybe you need to change your life?"

But, this is all memorized psychobabble rhetoric. And thus, their options, though based in qualitative statistics and appropriate schooling, are no more valid than the individual who claims superiority based in a completely animalistic sense of *Self.*

Spiritual Judgment
Spiritual Judgment holds its own unique set of criteria and is perhaps more damning than any

other. I mean as soon spirituality or religion is involved than God comes into play. And, when God is active, then all of the promises or curses of heaven and hell are in motion. And, due to the childhood programming instilled in most of us born into the western culture, mess with God or his servants and we are screwed.

How many times have those who hold the power in spiritual circles told people to do something and those people then believed it simply because they were told the speaking individual was a vessel of God and what they spoke was the words of God? To hear this, you may say, *"Come on. I would never believe that kind of nonsense!"* But, look around you. How many people that you know go to church, belong to a religious study group, have become Buddhist, Muslims, Born Again Christians, whatever… Simply because they were seeking a more fulfilled life and a connection to God or the Buddha?

The fact is, people are lost. They seek interpersonal interaction with others. And when the promises of religion come knocking at the door, they jump at the promises.

Many of these people become a part of the religious society for a time and then fall away. Others become deeply involved and become Priests, *Swamis,* Nuns, Monks, Yogis, or just generalized members of a cult.

Now there is nothing wrong with any of these things. This is your life and you can do whatever you want with it. Society may tell you a cult is bad. But, if it makes you happy, who is really to say that what you are doing anything wrong?

It is simply that at this level of personal interaction, *"A Member,"* begins to hand their life over to the person or persons in control. And, by doing that, one relinquishes control and thereby removes them self away from the path to true inner self-knowledge. This is the case, even though most religious group detail that one must totally give themselves over to the leader if they wish to truly interact with God and the divine aspects of this universe.

But, isn't any leader of a group simply dominated by the, *"I am more than you,"* mentality?

At the heart of unconscious human existence is the need to be more, excel, overpower, criticize others, and teach. Somehow in modern society *The Bigger* are always defined as *The Better.*

Many will say, *"Well that is the way of the world."* And, they are right. One would think that by being spiritual, however, there would be a way to step back from the controlling worldly-hands of power, control, judgment, and the need to be MORE. And, to a certain degree there is—one can go deeply into their mind, withdraw from other people, and completely remove themselves from this material world. In fact, this is why *yogis* have gone off to caves since the beginning of time—to remove themselves from the ways of the world.

This escapist ideology has always presented a problem, however. Because by escaping you may, in fact, come to control your personal mind. But, life is designed as an Interactive Sport. And, this is particularly the case for those who walk *The Spiritual Path.*

What this means is that not only must you find a way to come into harmony with the spiritual energies of the universe and nature, but also with man. (And, I use *"Man"* as a generic term). The problem is, with people there is judgment and conflict and the ideologies that MORE is always better.

Individual Creatures

We each are very individual creatures. We each have grown up in unique environments with unique personality traits, born form an individual set of experienced experiences. From this is born individual opinions, desires, and the way we each view and define the world.

Again, one may claim that simply by moving into a world of spirituality you can remove yourself from the controlling hands of the world to the degree that one can overcome these defining elements of life. But, can you?

You Are Who You Are

You are who you are! Just as each fingerprint or DNA is unique, so too is the essence of energy that emulates from you. Though spiritual and psychological reprogramming we can each redefine ourselves and how we interact with the world. But, at the root of humanity is personality. And, from personality comes conflict. No matter how spiritual you are.

Is this good or bad? I don't know. Because as I have long detail, good or bad is simply how you define it. *"If you love Hell it becomes Heaven."*

So, what do you do when the controlling hands of other people's desire for power, greed, and domination over you extend themselves? Well, you can go and get in a fight. Somebody comes at you, and you can argue your point until you're blue in the face. Or, you can go and kick their ass. There are a lot of problems with this, however, most notably the legal consequences.

162

Ultimately, personal interaction is based on conflict. It is defined by who can win the battle.

How is a battle won? It is won by the person who refuses to stop until they have overpowered the other person—either by words or by fists.

This is how cults drag people in. We all have things that we feel that are missing from our lives. That is just a by-product of human nature. The person involved in a cult (and I use the word, *"Cult,"* in most wide spanning definition, including accepted religious organizations) learns to talk to a person, ask the right questions, find what the person is missing, and then promise them an antidote.

Is this right? I don't know? But, it is how religious have gained new members since the dawn of time.

But, back to the point, at this level, the individual wins the conflict by bringing another sheep into the flock. Whether are not they believe what they are preaching and promising is true or not is almost unimportant, because they have conquered another life. They have won.

Desire

We can ultimately come to understand that all conflict is based in desire. All forms of seeking power over others are based in desire. People want to control others, so they go to school, they go to the seminary, they go to the gym and they learn how to fight, etc… What they are gaining at these places is a method for dominance. This is due to the fact that no matter what lie they are selling themselves, about why the doing what they are doing, studying what they are studying, they ultimately want to be MORE. MORE than other people.

The fact is, all level of individual unhappiness is based in desire. If you don't want anything else, then how can anyone sway you in any direction? And, if you are content in yourself, then you have no desire to gain control or have the need to feel empowered by being MORE than any other individual.

As desire can be understood to be the controlling dominant in all those who wish to be MORE. If you simply do not play the game, then no one wins and no one losses and perfect *karma* is set in motion.

BE. Do what you do. Let others do what they do. And, the controlling hands of words and people who seek to be MORE will have no effect upon you.

LET GO! And, you are free.

Chapter 15
The Dynamics of Transition

The Dynamics of Transition is one of the most crucial elements of conscious human existence. Transition can be defined as passing from one stage or moment of your life onto the next. Transition can be a very conscious process. Or, as is most often the case, it can become a forced passageway that is not calculated, hoped, or planned for.

The Witness

The Buddhist practitioner is trained to develop the ability to consciously step back from themselves and view all factors of their life. This process is called differing things by different schools of thought. Perhaps it is best defined as developing, *"The Witness."*

The Witness is you stepping back from you and observing what you are doing, why you are doing it, what you are feeling, and why you are feeling it. The techniques for the development of this level of consciousness are not some advanced forms of meditation that you must be initiated into for it to become fully actualized. It is simply you becoming very conscious of you.

This is a very necessary step on *The Spiritual Path*. Particularly in this fast-paced material world, where life changes in an instant, driven by any number of undefined reasons.

If you do not possess the ability to consciously witness yourself, you will not be able to make the changes or transitions that constantly occur in life from a perspective of consciousness. Instead, you will simply be thrown from one life melodrama onto the next and the next and the next.

How do you develop *The Witness?* Stop, Look, Listen. Don't make excuses for your actions. Don't judge your thoughts. Simply witness their existence. From this, you will define the basis of you.

Transition, Good or Bad

For those individuals who do not choose to refine their consciousness, each transition in life is defined only in its most elemental emotions: good or bad. Thus, the experiences of transition become only elemental determinants that one either ultimately loves or hates.

Life proves, to everyone who lives it, that it cannot be wholly calculated. Situations are going to occur that you did not anticipate or expect. Though many have attempted to live a shelter life to the degree that many of these random occurrences are eliminated, no doubt, sooner or later each person, no matter how protected, will encounter an unexpected rapid transition. This can occur from sickness, a physical accident, the oncoming death of a loved one, or even falling in love. From these, and so many other occurrences, one's life is set out of balance as all things are rapidly changed.

There are those who live their lives defined by such chaos that virtually every moment of their existence is delineated by unexpected occurrences, rapid, and unexpected transitions—both joyous and traumatic. These are the people who express their existence on a very rudimentary level and continually seek out arguments, confrontations, intoxication, lust, and even infatuation. To this type of individual, the constant roller coaster of experience comes to be an addiction—where they are constantly searching for the next adrenaline rush of experience.

No particular lifestyle, including the spiritual, is absent from this type of individual. Some, so called, *"Spiritual,"* individuals love to believe and, in fact, argue that their religion, their spiritual teacher, their form of meditation, is superior to all others. This is done simply to cause the controversy necessary for them to get their next adrenaline rush.

What occurs from a life lived at this level is that one is thrust into the world of winning and losing. Loss and gain equals emotional disruption. Emotional disruption is the pathway to a life void of enlightenment.

On the other side of the coin, there are those who are so sedentary in their ways that the moment even the slightest change occurs they are thrust into a world of not knowing what to do. Thus, the world of even mild transition becomes chaos to them.

From the perspective of Zen, we understand that life is a pathway. On any pathway there will be hills and valleys. How you climb the hill and descend into the valleys will delineate how conscious your pathway is towards enlightenment.

At the basis of your conscious transition is your ability to witness yourself. From this, you gained personal understand.

Wants and Desires

From personal understand, you can transcend the selfish wants and desires of your human form and move to a more refined space of consciousness where you are not solely driven by what you want, what you desire. Instead, you become sensitive and interactive with the needs of others and the universe around you.

How does this effect transition? By giving you the ability not to struggle. But, to accept the ever-changing nature of life.

The Acts of Others

Often times, transitions are brought on by the acts of others. Though we may not like another person's actions. In Zen we understand that, *"Life is perfect."* And that, the only thing that makes us lose this understanding of perfection, is personal desire—the desires for things to be different than they are.

Thus, by knowing yourself, accepting other, accepting that life is perfect, your path through transitional change becomes a natural process, possessing no boundaries.

Daily Transitions

Every day we each experience numerous transitions in our life. Most of these are must less traumatic than the aforementioned life-altering occurrence. Waking up is a transition. This process takes us from the ethereal world of dreams; to this place we call reality. Leaving your house to go to work, go shopping, or to visit a friend is a transition. What occurs is that you move from the enclosed safety of your abode to an external world where anything can happen.

Coming home from an outing is a transition. You move from the seeming chaos of the external world and reenter your realm of relative safety.

Sitting to meditate is a transition. You sit down, stop your random thoughts, and begin to focus your mind.

Standing up from a seated position is also a transition. Your body was at rest, now it must support itself with muscle strength.

All of these actions are transitions. Most people, however, never give them any thought. This is where the person of consciousness differs from the person of the world—they take the time to realize that each of these simply acts effects the passageway of life.

If you wake up and jump out of bed in a groggy, half-asleep state, your physical and mental actions will not be performed with any sense of excellence. If you run out of your front door, giving your passageway no thought, you may run into the rain, be wearing winter clothing in the midst of summer, or smash into another individual who is approaching your home. If you rush in from your outdoor adventure, you may forget things in your car, step on your cat, or forget to close your front door.

If you sit to meditate without proper preparation, your thoughts will run rapid and they will drive you to fantasies and the reliving of past situations and hopes for future events. If you jump up from a seated position, you may injure your knees or cause blood to rush from your head that will make you see stars.

All of these things can be avoided. Simply move slowly and experience the transition. Take your time to change from one state of mind to the next, one physical location to another. Do this no matter how seemingly mundane your physical or mental action may appear.

Experience

Experience the space you are in now. Experience as you move to your next space. Experience the new space once you get there. And, don't rush.

Conscious transition is the pathway to Nirvana.

Chapter 16
Magical Thinking

It is very easy to fall into the pattern of *Magical Thinking*. This is particularly the case for those of us who walk upon *The Spiritual Path*.

Spirituality goes *hand-in-hand* with the belief there is, *Karma*, a cosmic order to the universe, and that you may call upon mystical ethereal beings, God, or even the essence of the Buddha for assistance in times of need. Though this mindset has certainly been a byproduct of spirituality, this style of thinking is much more detrimental to the individual on the path to realization than it is an aid. This is primarily because of the fact that people who turn to this level of consciousness continually relinquish control of their lives to undefined, intangible, beings.

When one holds the belief that they may call upon these mystical entities for assistance, when life is not going according to desired plan, they separate themselves from the ever-evolving perfection of the universe. At the heart of Zen is accepting the perfection—everything is as it should be. Thus, by desiring things to be different than they are, you are choosing to separate yourself from Zen.

Moreover, when one calls upon these mystical beings for assistance and the undesirable patterns of life change, they believe that a miracle has occurred and that they, through prayer or mental focus, have caused life to be altered. On the other hand, when assistance is asked for and is not received, the individual becomes angry that their prayers were not met.

Where your prayers answered or not answered or was the perfection of life simply allowed to take its course?

Each person who delves into this realm of consciousness does so in their own unique manner. There is not an exact, singular, method for coming into contact with the ethereal realms. Prayer has certainly been a vehicle, as has visualization, and, in fact, crying, yelling, or screaming to God. In each of these examples, the person who is performing the action is basing their yearning upon desire—desire for things to be different than they are. As the Buddha said, *"The cause of suffering is desire."*

Each religion delineates their own set of standards and definitions to these entities. However, each religion generally details that the belief of another religion is mere superstition—their belief is the only belief—their faith, the only faith.

What we can conclude from this is that belief and faith to one person is superstition to another. Thus, the basis for *Magical Thinking* is not based in the realms of absolute certainty.

Many proponents of various forms of spirituality dictate that you should expect good things to happen to you—visualizing that the money you need will come, the parking space will be there when you arrive, or the person to help you will miraculously appear in your time of need. Though this is a great form of positive reaffirmation and cannot be criticized, most people take this mindset to the next level and become angry when their desires or needs are not fulfilled. Thus, this practice robs them of internal peace.

The next level of mental focus, which is commonly employed by the individual who follows the path of *Magical Thinking* is to focus upon what they want to the degree that it is brought into their lives. The great modern India sage, Swami Sivananada, detailed that for those who practice this type of *Magical Thinking* they may, in fact, receive what they desire but they will be controlled by the *Devis, "Ethereal goddesses,"* for their entire life and never be able to break away.

Certainly, each spiritual tradition and teacher approaches the subject of *Magical Thinking* with separate conclusions. What can be deduced, however, is that *Magical Thinking* removes you from the moment. It takes you away from relaxing into the fact this universe is perfect. If it were not perfect, how could all the inter-linking elements of creation be functioning in such a universal harmony. If the universe is in a function harmony, you as a human component of this universe must also be function in unseen accord. As such, everything that happens to you, whether you experience it as good or bad, is occurring for a reason and leading to a greater good.

If you can embrace this knowledge, then you will understand that even the experiences you viewed as negative have led you to the point in your life where you are today. Without them, you would not be the person you are.

If you hold onto the subjective negativity of any experience, then you allow it to control your mind for as long as it holds a place in your thoughts. Thus, the conveyor of these experiences maintains control over you indefinitely.

On-the-other-hand, if you witness the perfection, seeing all that is and all that has occurred as a pathway leading you closer and closer to realization that you have freed yourself from the concept of good and bad. Thus, not only are you free from the controlling hands of desire, but you are not bound to, *"Desire Consciousness,"* which make you demand that things be provided for you, given to you, and manifested upon your visualizations and prayers.

Living free from desire for things to be different than they actually are, you have left behind the need for *Magical Thinking*. Leaving behind *Magical Thinking* you enter *the Here and the Now*. *The Here and the Now* is where Zen is experienced.

Let go and know...

Chapter 17
The Student Becomes the Master

There is the tradition on the Buddhist path that one is a direct reflection of their teacher—that one possesses no authenticity unless they can document the transmission of enlightenment from their teacher to themselves and from their teacher to their teacher's teacher, back to the Buddha. Though this method of transmission is commonly accepted, there are many flaws in this path to enlightenment.

First, and perhaps most important, is the fact that enlightenment is not something which can be given. Enlightenment is not a rank that can be earned. Enlightenment is a personal process of progressing towards the ultimate understanding of human consciousness. Though a teacher is commonly used as a tool to lay the foundations that ultimately achieve this end, a teacher cannot give you *Nirvana* as if it were some sort of gift or an earned distinction.

Student consciousness is obvious throughout *the Spiritual Path*. When one is initially drawn to the path, the first step is oftentimes the seeking of a *Guru*. Once one becomes a disciple, they often times idolize this individual to the degree that they believe them to be so all encompassingly holy that obtaining their level of consciousness is a virtual impossibility. Due to this fact, students become locked into, *"Disciple Consciousness."* Though they become great at performing the techniques of worship, they do not develop the necessary mental elements to let go of this limited understanding and move onto the realm where *Nirvana* may actually be embraced.

Christians are the ideal example of, *"Disciple Consciousness."* They have attached such a great singular obtainment to one figure, Jesus Christ, that how could anyone ever hope to become, *"The Son of God?"* What is misunderstood by many modern Christians and is revealed by Middle East, Judaic, and Biblical scholars is that the term, *"Son of God,"* or more precisely translated, *"Child of God,"* was a term that was assigned to everyone from the Jewish faith of that era that were persecuted by the Romans. As time evolved and translations of the writing of the disciples of Jesus took place, the term *"Son of God"* took on the singular connation of being assigned solely to Jesus Christ.

When an ideology becomes singularly obtained by one individual, it obviously cannot be experienced by any other person. Buddhism is no different.

Siddhartha Guatama, The Sakyamuni Buddha, lived over two thousand years ago. Numerous legends have come to be attributed to his life and his enlightenment. With a being so distant and so immaculate, how can anyone hope to achieve the same level of consciousness?

Whereas Christianity has evolved to the level where it is, in fact, blasphemy to contradict the totality of holiness that is solely held by Jesus Christ, the Buddhist should not be bound by this mentality. Yet, in many cases, they are.

Certainly, from a Christian perspective, it may be argued that, *"Enlightenment is not God-hood."* But, it must be kept in mind that the Buddhist does not want to become the, *"Son of God."* The Buddhist seeks enlightenment: oneness between *the Individual Self, the Universal Self,* and *the Cosmic Whole.*

In India, where Buddha found his enlightenment, there are an untold number of *Sadhus, Yogis,* and *Renunciates* everywhere. They do the most abstract things to their body and mind in order to alter their consciousness so that enlightenment may enter. They vow to stand only on one leg for a lifetime. They walk naked through the streets, never wearing any clothing, even in the cold of the Himalayan winter. They lock themselves away in caves, refusing to interact with any other human being. This is all done as a pathway to enlightenment. Though these beings may have been initially initiated by a *Guru*, who gave them a mantra or a specific spiritual practice, they have let go of *"Disciple Consciousness,"* and have forged their won pathway to *Nirvana.*

Legend states that Buddha himself had two primary teachers. But, he found no enlightenment from either of them. So, he moved forward and achieved *Nirvana* by his own method.

Immaculate Connotations

Whatever immaculate connotation you assign to your teacher, it is must be understood that as long as you unduly idolize them, you will never reach *Nirvana. Nirvana* can only be experienced by the individual who let's go of the definitions of, *"Better and Worse," "Higher and Lower," "Less and More,"* and relinquishes themselves to the fact by letting go you can become one with all that is: nature, the teacher, and the universe. This is *Nirvana.*

The Pali Canon of Buddhism describes twenty-eight Buddha that lived before Siddhartha Guatama. Throughout the centuries in India, Nepal, Tibet, Thailand, Japan, and now the Western World, there have been cases of others who have also achieved the highest level of consciousness. So, it is doable! But, it is ultimately only doable by you.

Do you wish to be a student or do you wish to be enlightened? If you say you are not good enough, knowledgeable enough, pure enough, or holy enough—you never will be. Your teacher may know more than you, but that is information and knowledge. Information and knowledge are nice, they are even useful to present a point of view, but they are not enlightenment. Enlightenment is steeping beyond all that is believed and that is known.

Let go of your teacher and become enlightenment.

Chapter 18
Don't Get Lost in the Tranquility

The concept of meditation has been indoctrinated into the Western mind for many decades. Certainly, the vast influx of Eastern Spirituality that came *hand-in-hand* with the Beat and the Hippie Generations spread this understanding throughout Western Society.

Virtually everyone has heard of meditation, and most are taught that meditation is a process where the mind is calmed, blood pressured is lowered, and the practitioner emerges more tranquil. All of these factors are definitely a byproduct of the elementary realms of meditation. As such, many medical doctors prescribe classed in yoga and meditation to their patients who are feeling stressed out or anxiety ridden from the tolls of modern life. These prescribing doctors, for the most part, have never practiced meditation, however. If they have, it was only at the most superficial level. And, perhaps there lies the problem with the dissemination of meditation that has taken place in the Western world; its true purpose is completely misunderstood.

During the 1960's the concept of meditation spread throughout the west. There was yoga and meditation classes taught everywhere. This phenomenon continued into the 1970's. With this early propagation of meditation came very large groups such as *Transcendental Meditation* whose figurehead Maharishi Mahesh Yogi lead the masses into the meditative mindset.

In TM, the practitioner is taught to meditate for a few minutes, two times a day. What occurred with the widespread dissemination of TM, however, is that the meditation practitioner, who was only willing to practice for a few minutes a day, had the seal of approval from a true *East Indian Yogi. "If Maharishi Mahesh Yogi says this is meditation, then it must be meditation—right?"*

Now, there is certainly nothing wrong with TM, or any other Westernized form of meditation which guides the practitioner to perform the practice for only a few minutes a day. In fact, it can help many people reduce the stress in their life and cause their mind to become more centered. The problem is, with this widespread decimation of Westernized meditation the true purpose of meditation has been not only redefined by Western society, but its true essence has been lost, as well. Thus, the true essence of meditation is being forgotten.

Walking the Spiritual Path

For those who walk *The Spiritual Path* and practice meditation in its more refined form, there is an additional element that has caused the practitioner to miss the true point and principal of the practice of meditation. This subtle element is tranquility.

While practicing meditation, in its more refined forms, a sensation occurs in the practitioner. It is a sense of supreme tranquility. The problem is, however, it feels so great—the tranquility is so permeating, that many practitioners become lost in this feeling. When they meditate, they meditate to re-experience this sensation. Though it feels great, this is also not the ultimate reason for practicing meditation.

What is Meditation?

Meditation was formalized many centuries ago as a means to bring the practitioner into communion with the divine essence of this universe. Throughout the centuries there have been a few pivotal figures that have guided the process of meditation to new levels of excellence—whereby the practitioner could delve into this process while achieving accelerated results. Siddhartha Guatama, the Sakyamuni Buddha and Sri Shankaracharya were two ideal examples of living beings that redefined the process of meditation.

It must be understood, however, that meditation is elementally not about simply chilling-out. It is a process that directs the practitioner to divine communication. Therefore, if it is practiced for any other reason, though its effects may be beneficial to the *Self,* the *Divine Self* will not be revealed.

Now here lies one of the essential problems with meditation. If it is practiced to achieve an end result; i.e.: peace, calm, or even enlightenment, then that end result will never be known. I am sure this sound very Zen to many of you, but bear with me...

The spiritual person lives their life at a level that is never embraced by the common person. Everything they do, they do for the spiritual essence of the universe. They commonly practice *Karma Yoga, "The yoga of selfless service,"* the pray, they meditate, they whatever... But, all that they do is done in order to bring about a harmony of body, mind, self, and universe.

Here again, this is one of the complicated, subtle points of spiritual existence. The spiritual practitioner is locked in a human form. As such, they have desires, wants, and needs. But, for the person who walks upon *the Spiritual Path*, these wants and desires are geared towards personal and universal consciousness.

Without the *Self* there can be *No Self.* Without the *Unknowing* there can be no *Knowing.* To this end, the spiritual practitioner walks a very subtle road of constantly redefining what is spiritual and what is not. Thus, they use meditation as a means to bring *Self* into contact with *Universal Self,* thereby revealing what is truly *Real.*

The Early Path

When one enters *The Spiritual Path*, they are commonly very enthusiastic about their decision to move down this road. They constantly talk about what they believe to be spiritual, how holy their *Guru* is, and how they are truly practicing meditation. Most, however, soon fall away from *The Spiritual Path*. This is human nature.

People want to be, *"Something."* Thus, they become doctors, lawyers, teachers, truck drivers, policemen, and holy men. But, this, *"Being,"* is the exact opposite of, *"Truly Being."*

The Bodhisattva Vow

In Buddhism, there is *the Vow of the Bodhisattva.* This is the vow that a practitioner takes which states that he or she will continue to reincarnate, come back to this place we call life, even after they reach enlightenment, in order to help the masses, reach that perfect plateau of human existence, *Nirvana.*

Now, as nice and as selfless as all this sound, *the Vow of the Bodhisattva* is all about ego. It is all about, *"I."* This is where the person walking *The Spiritual Path* truly gets sidetracked. If you lock into,

"I," then your path and your meditation are meaningless. *"I,"* keeps enlightenment from ever being allowed to occur.

Why? *"I,"* separates you from the divine. Therefore, if anything that you do while walking *the Spiritual Path* is about, *"I,"* whether it being thinking that you have something to give, something to teach, something to say, or the ability to cause yourself to reincarnate to save all of humanity, you are totally lost. At no level is enlightenment about, *"I."* In fact, at no level is meditation about, *"I."*

If you are thinking, *"I am meditating,"* you are not! If you are thinking, *"My meditation is getting deeper,"* it is not!

Let's Get Subtle Again

Let's get subtle again... Life is life. We are in a human body. We do human things. And, we want human things. Wanting in natural.

Monks, Priests, Nuns, and Swamis, for centuries, have attempted to shelter themselves from the world in order to curtail their wants. But, what did it prove?

What they did was all about, *"I."* They wanted something! They wanted enlightenment. They wanted to know God. They wanted to be remembered as a saint.

Go to India—especially in the holy cities of Rishikesh or Hardwar, and you will see people all over the place standing on one leg for the rest of their life, walking around naked, ceasing to speak, chanting mantras constantly, etc., etc., etc. All claiming what they do is a means of meditation—a pathway to God.

Go to the Philippines during the Christian holy times and you will see people actually putting crowns of thorns on their heads and being nailed to a cross. But, what does all this prove?

What it proves is that the people who do these things are locked into, *"I." "I am doing this because..."*

"Because," is not about spiritually. *Because* is only about *Because. Because* is based in ego. *Because* is based in the personal belief of how one person believes this place we call, *"Life,"* is supposed to operate.

In India, if someone had not previously described that deciding to stand on one leg for the rest of their existence was holy, do you think that someone would simply decide to do it? No. In the Philippines, if Jesus had not been nailed to the cross, do you think that anyone would simply decide, *"Hey, why don't you nail me to a cross?"* No.

Meditative holiness has been removed from the essence of spirituality and all that remains is tradition. It is due to this fact people define enlightenment as a, *"Thing,"* and a, *"Place,"* to get to.

As long as you define enlightenment as a *"Thing,"* or a *"Place,"* it can never be known. This is the point where some very insightful Zen Buddhist decided to begin breaking thought the vail of all the nonsense and detail, *"We are all enlightened. All you have to do is remember it."*

Back to Meditation

Here is where we get back to the root point and the true essence of meditation...

Now, listen carefully, *"If you are using meditation as a tool, meditation becomes meaningless. Yes, it may calm you down and lower your blood pressure. But, it will not show you the deeper realms of Universal Self."*

So often I hear people say that, *"My meditation is a step-by-step process."* Or, *"I am making little steps towards enlightenment by meditating."*

If enlightenment was a curriculum at a university, then you could actually make steps towards earning your degree. But, enlightenment is *Here.* Enlightenment is *Now.* To know it, you must give up the process—including meditation. For in the *Zero* and the *Emptiness* is the only place enlightenment can be found.

Chapter 19
The Pathway to Enlightenment

I frequently write and speak about enlightenment. I explain that we all are enlightened; we simply must embrace this consciousness and remember this fact. From this, I receive an untold number of questions about just what do I mean? Many people come up to me with the statements, *"I'm not enlightened, but I want to be." "I have practiced meditation for many years, and I still don't feel enlightened."* Or, *"I can never be as enlightened as my Guru."*

To hopefully clear a few things up for those who walk *The Spiritual Path* it must initially be detailed that first of all enlightenment is not about desire. If you desire enlightenment, you will never know enlightenment.

Secondarily, meditation is not a pathway to enlightenment—though many teachers throughout the centuries have claimed that it is. Meditation is a, *"Mind Thing."* It is a great tool to calm the mind and bring you into communion with your inner self and the God that resides in you. But, it will not provide you with enlightenment.

And finally, you cannot find enlightenment by following a teacher. Though teachers may guide you to higher consciousness, ultimately, *"Following"* keeps you from enlightenment—as you are defining your own cosmic understanding by that of your teachers.

"Okay," you say, *"Then just what is the pathway to enlightenment if you can't want it,*

practice for it, or study to obtain it?" Well, first of all to comprehend the answer, the essence of enlightenment must to be understood.

Depicting Enlightenment

Most people, those who are unenlightened, depict enlightenment as a mystical abstract thing that can be had. But, anyone who believes this incorrect ideology is entirely missing the point. Enlightenment cannot be had. Because if it can be had, that means it is missing in you. If it is missing in you, then it is not a natural occurrence and should not be sought after anyway.

Enlightenment is. Thus, it is never something to gain.

Many teachers also detail that you must possess a certain level of high incarnation to gain enlightenment. Teachers, who detail this fact, also state that it will take you many incarnations to even come close to embracing enlightenment.

By stating this, they immediately prove that they do not understand enlightenment and are, in fact, completely keeping their students from ever embracing the naturalness of enlightenment.

Now certainly, it is much easier for a person to embrace the total-ness of enlightenment if they are walking *The Spiritual Path*—because those who walk *The Spiritual Path* have a rudimentary understanding of enlightenment and what to expect. This is not to say, however, that anyone, *everyone,* cannot know enlightenment. Because, if it was only available to those who walked *The Spiritual Path,* who embrace this sense of pure consciousness, then one would have to be spiritual to know.

But, being spiritual is not the defining factor of enlightenment. Being whole is.

This is all very Zen, I understand. But, let me make it more understandable. When I first heard Ram Dass detailing that his *Guru,* Neem Karoli Baba had gone *eye-to-eye* with him and asked him, *"Don't you see everything is perfect,"* it really touched a place in me. Yes, all the good and even all of the bad in this life is perfect. It all happens in accordance with its own perfection.

Life is Life

Now, a Christian may say the good is a gift from God and the bad is a test. But, they are really missing the point. Good and Bad are simply points of view. *If you love Hell, then it becomes Heaven.*

What I am saying is that you cannot gage life. You cannot say that one particular experience that you felt that was very negative may not lead you onto a very new and positive place of growth and personal understanding.

Life is Life and things are going to happen that we do not like. But, if you can step back long enough to embrace a divine understanding, they you can see that this action leads to the next and the next and the next.

If you lay a positive pathway for your life— not hurting, criticizing, or demeaning others, then from the nature of this universe, you attract positive energy.

Additionally, just the opposite is true if you live in space of unhappiness, where you place yourself at constant odds against the world around you—if you embrace negativity, no matter how subtle, then negativity will find you and bad things will occur.

Now, what does this have to do with enlightenment you ask? It has everything to do with enlightenment.

Enlightenment is about you accepting the perfection of the moment. If you are criticizing, judging, (be it good or bad), or measuring your amount of *"Feel Good-ness"* in a particular moment of life, then you are setting yourself at odds with the perfection of the universe and you are keeping yourself from enlightenment.

Life is life. We like what we like. We don't like what we don't like. But, you cannot allow this to define you. It just is what it is.

Accept what you like as what you like, what you don't like as what you don't like. Know it, but do not allow it to control you, define you, or hold you back.

Understanding the perfection of the universe is not saying that God, Allah, or Buddha, is waving some controlling hand and making all of the elements occur. Understanding perfection is simple settling into the perfection and knowing that it all is as it is. This is, also, not to say that some *Supreme Being* made it that way. It just is.

When things just are, that is the root of enlightenment.

It is often detailed when a person dies that their life flashes before their eyes. Having been a person who has come very close to physical death a couple of times in my, *"Life-Time,"* I can categorically state that this statement is not true.

What occurs is that when you are at the gates of leaving your physical body, you immediately embrace the perfection. You see how this thought lead to that desire—how that desire led to this choice—how this choice led to that action—how this action led to this outcome. Ultimately, you see how all of life was perfect. How everything falls into its own space of perfection and you lived exactly what you were supposed to live—whether you liked every moment of it or not.

This is the source point for enlightenment. Initially understanding, then accepting, and finally embracing *The Perfection*.

Embrace the Perfection and know enlightenment.

Chapter 20
It's All in the Giving

Words are an interesting element of this place we call, *"Life."* Words are one of our primary means of communication. They express how we feel, what we are thinking, want we want, and how we want others to behave. Words are a seemingly necessary component of life. Yet, in India, there are many *Sadhus* who consciously give up the use of words, altogether, as one of their primary methods of *Sadhana.* Why do they do it? To gain control over their emotions and their desires.

Emotions... This is where words come to play an adversarial role in the development of human consciousness.

Many people have learned very early in their childhood that if they use words, actions, and sounds, in a very specific manner, they can gain control over those people around them. They find that if they yell and scream loud enough, they will get what they want.

Of course, adults who continue to use this technique do so from a very unconscious place in the spectrum of human consciousness. It rises from one of our most animalistic centers. *"I want this and if I behave in a specific way I will obtain it."*

This is the same source-point for people who immediately turn the tables in a verbal disagreement. If you are expressing your dissatisfaction with their thoughts or their actions, they immediately change the focus of the discussion and either get mad at you for being mad at them, or make you feel wrong or guilty for expressing your feelings. This too is a learned behavior and a means of controlling others. These actions are based in the fact that these individuals have learned subtle methods to gain control over others, leaving themselves free from the need to face their own objectionable actions and negative interpersonal interactions. Thereby, allowing their own personal desires to be the dominant force in any relationship.

These types of behavior are performed without consciousness of thought, however. They are simply a mastered reaction to life not going in the direction that a specific individual desires.

As these emotional outbursts or verbal manipulations are unleashed without thought, control, or prejudgment, then this style of action is lost to the realms of lack of consciousness. And, this is the space that each person who walks *The Spiritual Path* (or even those who simply wish to live life in a more refined manner) must avoid.

It must be understood that many worldly people will claim that they do not care about refined consciousness and/or how other people think or feel. With this as a basis, they believe they can act in any manner they deem fit. They are simply interested in the fact that they feel okay as much of the time and possible, and who cares what effect they are having on the lives of others.

Though this is a very common form of human existence, all those who live in that space eventually come to regret that they have unleashed such selfishness on the world. This is because of the fact that eventually, through time and through age, not only are they continually bombarded by negative *karma*, but they also end up alone and unloved, because no one wants to associate with them.

This is one of the finer points on the *Path of Human Consciousness;* though we all want what we want, we have to choose to be big enough to let go of desire in any given moment to serve the betterment of human evolution.

This understanding is what sets the individual on *the Spiritual Path* apart from those who solely embrace the ways of the world.

"But, why should they get what they want and not me?" Because this is human life. We place ourselves in Life Situations. Once we are in them, we have to be spiritually strong enough to accept what these situations present to us and live with that outcome.

To explain more clearly, life is based in desire. We want what we want. Some of us go after what we want; meaning we pursue our goals. By pursuing our goals, we are going to come into contact with other people. Commonly, as we pursue our goals, there will be those who have more experience, expertise, or power in a specific arena of life, and, thus, they may be the one who will ultimately get what they want in a given *Life-Circumstance.*

If we take a closer look at this, we can easily understand that this is why the person on *the Spiritual Path* very consciously leaves behind as many desires and emotions as possible. With fewer desires, not only are there less *Let-Downs* in life but there is also less circumstance where you will encounter situations where you do not receive what you had hoped for.

But, it is easy to say, *"Give up your desires and you will be free."* It is much harder to implement this understanding, however.

To do so, it must be understood that first of all, you must be very clear and precise in your desires and then pursue only the ones that you are willing to pay the price for their obtainment.

Because there is always a price to pay in life for everything!

Secondarily, you must accept every situation for what it is. You may not like it, but you must give in and accept it. With this, you will possess the initial tools to accept people and situations for what they are. Though you may not particularly like them, you will be able to learn from each person and occurrence and consciously become a more refined participant in life.

This is where the refined interaction with people comes into play in this equation. We all have had people come into our lives that have truly helped us. We meet some people and we are in awh of what they have given us. With others, it is subtler. It takes time to truly grasp what effect they have had upon our lives.

Now, here again, we must embrace the spiritual understanding of perception.

If we consciously free ourselves and are not dominated by what we may or may-not want from of any particular *Life-Event* or interaction, then we are free to experience what we can truly learn from each person and situation.

This is a subtle area of consciousness that needs to be understood. First of all, most people who walk through this place we call, *"Life," are* not devotees of consciousness. They travel from birth to death focused solely upon Self.

From a more refined perspective we can understand that this is not necessarily nice. But, the reality is, that is the condition of most inhabitants of this world.

From a spiritual understanding we must accept this fact and refine our own consciousness to the level that we are simply thankful for what each person we encounter has taught us. In many cases, the fact is; it is simply that we learn how not to behave and how not to live life.

Once we begin to exist in this conscious state of acceptance, we are allowed to move forward and do what we do with the refined understanding of, *"Learning from All."*

This is not to say that one should stay in negative relationships, be they on the personal or the group level. But, this is to say that we must accept the learning experiences that our choices have provided us with and grow from the understandings we gain from these interactions.

This takes us to the next level; from desire we learn how to do *Life-Things.* In some cases, we become masters of various life activities. With this, others may come to us, as it is their desire to learn or achieve what we have already accomplished. This is where life becomes a *Giving Opportunity.*

As I often state, the best teachers have been those who have never claimed to be teachers. Those who claim to know are basing most of their conclusions on ego—not spiritual understanding. So, to truly give, to teach—one must consciously remove *Self* from the equation.

This is not an easy thing to do. When you go to someone to learn you are in a willing state. But, to give and to teach from that same state of selflessness takes refined clarity of mind and heart.

But, this is what *The Spiritual Path* is truly all about. It is not about becoming, *"Personally-More"* or *"Individually-Greater."* It is about making all of this *Life-Space* more and greater. It is about the *Common-Good.*

As each of us gets older, we gain more and more knowledge and insight about the varying aspects of life. Through our *karma*, destiny, and desires we enter into various Life-Places and we eventually emerging with knowledge that others do not yet possess. From here we are each able to pass on this knowledge to others who can then expand upon it. But, this teaching must be done from a space of *Pure-Heart.* Only then does the teacher truly embrace the understanding that, *"Life is all about giving."*

"Giving" must be understood before you run out onto the highway of life and believe that you are doing the right thing.

Each of us has encountered people in our lives who thought they knew what was best for us. Whether this has been family, friends, or religion, we each have been told what others believe we should be doing with our lives. In some cases, these people were right. In most cases, however, they were not. This simple fact teaches us that no one can ever truly know what is right for another person. Therefore, we can never enter *The Path of Giving* believing that we are going to make another person's life better by what we have to offer or what we think that they need.

Ultimately, no one can tell you what is right for you. You are you. It is only you who can decide. And, this is the source-point for one of the greatest elements of human-life, *Free-Will.*

You can decide to do whatever you want to do with your life. Whether or not what you are doing is adding to the overall good. Certainly, religion and politics have destroyed millions of lives. These actions have been implemented by those people, in positions of power, believing that their way is the only way, that they know more than others, or that they have something to give that someone else needs. But, look at the outcome. And, this is where the refinement of your *Free-Will* must come into play.

The individual on *The Spiritual Path* consciously avoids the conflict of mind, ego, and desire in giving. They are never so foolish to believe that they think that they know what another person needs. They live in a world where giving comes from a state of refined consciousness, not misplace desire.

You know what is right. You know what is wrong. This is another of the great-elements of human-life. The trick is to not allow your *Self* to be harnessed by desires that will make you do bad things to achieve your own misplaced desired end-results, and do them with the false premise of, *"Giving."*

That is not giving. That is not caring. That is simply desire and control.

Giving is never about breaking or destroying. Giving is about fixing and making all-things better.

Giving is about making every *Life-Situation* you enter into better for your having been there. Giving is about leaving every place you enter, better, not worse.

On the most simplistic level of this understanding, you can clean up messes you find that have been created by other people. You can help people when they are in need of help, instead of simply walking by and thinking, *"I haven't got time for that."*

Giving means that if you have done bad things in the past, spoken negatively about an individual, or performed negative actions that have adversely affected others, that you do all that you can to correct the negativity that you have unleashed and never give up until what negative events you have created are repaired. Giving is about fixing what you have broken!

Ultimately, giving is about the giving up of you. Just like the *Sadhu* who gives up speech to make himself or herself a more *whole-ly* and conscious person, giving is not about giving something that that you what to give, or something that you think another person needs. Giving is about putting yourself away and giving everything—placing all you have in the supreme whole of perfection and letting whomever wants to partake receive your everything.

Giving is *the Path of Consciousness.* Giving is the road to a better life and a better world.

Give what you have to give. Desire nothing in return: no thanks, no gifts, no fame, no love, no friendship, no good *karma.* Then, you are giving from a pure-space and the world around you instantly becomes a better place.

Give without Desire. This is true Spirituality

Do Right. Live Right. Give.

THE ZEN

www.ingramcontent.com/pod-product-compliance
Lightning Source LLC
Chambersburg PA
CBHW072002090426
42740CB00011B/2051